Revival of
the Bible

A Fresh Look at the Word of God

Revival of the Bible

A Fresh Look at the Word of God

BY
SARAH BOWLING

Harrison House
Tulsa, OK

05 04 03 02 01   10 9 8 7 6 5 4 3 2 1

Revival of the Bible:
A Fresh Look at the Word of God
ISBN 1-57794-381-3
Copyright © 2001 by Sarah Bowling
P.O. Box 17340
Denver, CO 80217

Published by Harrison House, Inc.
P.O. Box 35035
Tulsa, Oklahoma 74153

Contents

Preface

As you read this book, let God work in your heart in a progressive way. Isaiah 28:10 says, "precept upon precept, line upon line, here a little, there a little."

If you're not reading your Bible daily, then I want to encourage you to let this book penetrate your daily routine to include some Bible time. If you're already reading your Bible daily, that's great! Let this book encourage this habit so it will become a permanent lifestyle. Perhaps you'll also begin to allow God to challenge you through these pages to go deeper with Him into His Word.

Whatever your present relationship with God's Word, God has great things for you in this book!

Acknowledgments

I'd like to thank my husband for his invaluable support in helping me achieve God's destiny for my life.

I'd also like to thank my mom for continually pointing me to the Bible throughout my life.

Last, and most important, I'd like to thank God, who has enabled me to join in His amazing plan for this planet!

Introduction

Generation after generation, man's primary pursuit in life has been a search for "meaning." Every human being seeks, in one form or fashion, to discover his or her purpose for living. The search takes many forms—education, religion, drug and alcohol abuse—but the root cause of the quest is the same. We want to know why we are here. What were we made for?

Ultimately, the meaning and purpose we seek can be found in only one place—the Bible. God has given us the Bible as a manual for living. He uses His written Word to illustrate His love for us, lead us to our purpose in life, and provide us with the wisdom, comfort, and encouragement we need every day.

How do we utilize this gift of God's Word? We must spend time reading, memorizing, and meditating on it. Through God's Word, we will learn how to recognize God's voice in the many ways He speaks to us. God's Word will show us our purpose in life and give us the strength and the wisdom we need to combat the lies that would seek to extinguish that purpose.

My goal in writing this book is to help you discover and enjoy the amazing benefits of God's Word. The Bible is relevant to every area of your life:

- The Bible demonstrates God's love for you.

- The Bible is God's primary way of speaking to you.

- The Bible defines your purpose in life.

- The Bible gives you the wisdom and strength to overcome the lies that can extinguish your purpose.

This book was designed to be very user-friendly and interactive. You will learn why and how you should meditate on God's Word and you'll find lists of Scriptures that will guide you in your meditation. You will also find tips on carving out a quiet time, memorizing Scripture, reading your Bible, and much more. You will learn who you are in God's economy and why you're on the planet. You will learn how to easily identify and combat the lies that would try to extinguish your purpose. And you will learn, through biblical examples, how God's principles apply to your daily life.

Before we can move on to all that, the first step in making the Bible relevant to your life is knowing Jesus. Jesus is the Word of God made flesh.

John 1:1 and 14 NLT say:

In the beginning the Word already existed. He was with God, and he was God.

So the Word became human and lived here on earth among us. He was full of unfailing love and faithfulness.

Why do you need Jesus? Through Adam, every person born has the sin nature, but Jesus died to free you from sin and justify you before God. When you accept Jesus' work on the cross, God sees you "in" Jesus.

In Adam all die, even so in Christ all shall be made alive.

■ I CORINTHIANS 15:22

Why can you have Jesus? God's love for you is so great that He sent Jesus to pay the price for your sin. Jesus' death, burial, and resurrection provided you a way to God.

This is how much God loved the world: He gave his Son, his one and only Son. And this is why: so that no one need be destroyed; by believing in him, anyone can have a whole and lasting life.

■ JOHN 3:16 MESSAGE

If you are not already born again and walking in fellowship with Jesus, or if you're just not sure of your standing with God, I would like for you to pray the following prayer out loud.

Prayer for Salvation

Dear Heavenly Father,

Thank You for bringing this book across my path. I am a sinner. I recognize and acknowledge my need for Jesus. I ask You, Jesus, to come into my heart and wash away my sin. I confess that You died for my sin, You were buried, and God raised You from the dead. Thank You for becoming my personal Lord and Savior. I want to begin a relationship with You today.

In Jesus' name, amen.

Now that you've taken that essential step, God's Word can become alive and relevant in your life. You can truly experience a *Revival of the Bible!*

Section One:

Bible Basics

Chapter One

Why Do I Need a Revival of the Bible?

WHAT IS REVIVAL?

revival (ri v_'vel), n. 1. the act of reviving or state of being revived. 2. restoration to life or vigor. 3. restoration to use or acceptance.[1]

Above are the first three out of the five definitions for *revival* listed in *Webster's Desk Dictionary of the English Language*. I've listed those three because they each apply to the purpose of *Revival of the Bible*.

> *1. the act of reviving or state of being revived*

I want this book to act as a catalyst in reviving your heart. Whether you are a new believer, or you've been a believer for years, the Bible should be central to your daily life. Spending time reading and meditating on God's Word is not a means of salvation but a way to understand everything salvation means.

The Bible is unlike any book you've ever read. God's Word is alive and its depths have yet to be discovered. For hundreds of years men have written volume after volume about the Bible, from books as broad in scope as the entire Bible to books focused on only a few verses, but there is always something fresh to be found.

Therefore, my primary goal is to spark a revival in your heart. I want to be in "the act of reviving" you throughout the pages of this book so that you will be in the "state of being revived."

2. *restoration to life or vigor*

The everyday hassles in life have the potential to zap your last ounce of energy. Going to God's Word on a daily basis to find strength and encouragement is like receiving a daily shot in the arm. As you read this book, ask God to renew your hunger for His Word. Then satisfy that hunger by spending time in the Bible. Allowing that revival to take place in your heart will "restore your life and vigor."

3. *restoration to use or acceptance*

This definition is perhaps a less personal one, but it is of vital importance to every believer. In the early years of public education in America, the Bible was a central part of every day's studies. It was the foundation for education. Many of the most prestigious universities in our country today were originally founded as Bible colleges or seminaries.

As the Bible has lost its prominence in our culture, we have witnessed a serious moral decline. As love for the Word of God is revived in your heart, pray that the Bible will be "restored to use and acceptance." Revival usually begins in the hearts of small groups of people who are dedicated to God's Word and prayer. As your hope is renewed and you learn your true purpose in life, let that revival start with you and ignite those around you.

WHY DO I NEED A REVIVAL OF THE BIBLE?

God's Word serves many functions in our daily Christian walk. It is necessary for spiritual growth, living free from sin, and living the abundant life God intended for us. It provides wisdom, strength, and comfort to face the challenges we meet every day. It corrects, admonishes, and disciplines us when we fall short; then it helps us to receive God's forgiveness and restoration.

The Bible can direct us and help us to focus on the things that are truly important in life. When you discover what's truly important, you won't feel so pressured and stressed by trivial things. You'll see your life from God's perspective. In view of eternity, getting cut off on the freeway isn't such a big deal.

Any lack in your life can be satisfied through God's Word. When you keep your focus on Him, you won't feel needy or lonely. And there may be times when you lose your focus—we all do—but God is always right there waiting for you to look His way again.

God has provided you this source of hope and wisdom because He is crazy about you. He loves you. He has chosen to use the Bible as His primary method of teaching you just how much He loves you.

But God demonstrates His own love toward us, in that while we were still sinners, Christ died for us.

■ ROMANS 5:8

The apostle Paul wrote to the Christians at the church in Ephesus to encourage them, as well as us today, to take studying the Bible and our relationship with God seriously, so that we may experience the depth of God's marvelous love.

> I pray that Christ will be more and more at home in your hearts as you trust in him. May your roots go down deep into the soil of God's marvelous love. And may you have the power to understand, as all God's people should, how wide, how long, how high, and how deep his love really is. May you experience the love of Christ, though it is so great you will never fully understand it. Then you will be filled with the fullness of life and power that comes from God.
>
> ■ EPHESIANS 3:17-19 NLT

The following verse emphasizes the awe-inspiring love God has toward us.

> Behold what manner of love the Father has bestowed on us, that we should be called children of God!
>
> ■ I JOHN 3:1

GOD'S LOVE SEEN THROUGHOUT THE BIBLE

The whole book of the Song of Solomon is an allegory of Christ's love for His bride, the church. Here in Nehemiah we see more of God's goodness toward each of us.

You are God, ready to pardon, gracious and merciful, slow to anger, abundant in kindness, and did not forsake them.

■ NEHEMIAH 9:17

The book of Psalms is an excellent place to read about His love, protection, guidance, and provision. If you have never discovered this wonderful book, I encourage you to spend some time there. These were originally written as songs to recall God's faithfulness in the writers' lives and to the nation of Israel.

You may want to consider highlighting each Psalm that praises God. They are encouraging to read during difficult times, or when you just need a lift.

There's much to be learned about God in the Psalms. Here are a few examples that show God's goodness and greatness. As you read, spend a few moments meditating, letting your mind think on the truths mentioned in each one.

Show Your marvelous lovingkindness by Your right hand, O You who save those who trust in You from those who rise up against them.

■ PSALM 17:7

He loves whatever is just and good, and his unfailing love fills the earth. But the Lord watches over those who fear him, those who rely on his unfailing love.

■ PSALM 33:5,18 NLT

God's love is meteoric, his loyalty astronomic, his purpose titanic, his verdicts oceanic. Yet in his largeness nothing gets lost; not a man, not a mouse, slips through the cracks.

How exquisite your love, O God! How eager we are to run under your wings, to eat our fill at the banquet you spread as you fill our tankards with Eden spring water. You're a fountain of cascading light, and you open our eyes to light.

■ PSALM 36:5-9 MESSAGE

Because Your lovingkindness is better than life, my lips shall praise You.

■ PSALM 63:3

Blessed be God: he didn't turn a deaf ear, he stayed with me, loyal in his love.

■ PSALM 66:20 MESSAGE

O Lord, you are so good, so ready to forgive, so full of unfailing love for all who ask your aid. But you, O Lord, are a merciful and gracious God, slow to get angry, full of unfailing love and truth.

■ PSALM 86:5,15 NLT

For as the heavens are high above the earth, so great is His mercy toward those who fear Him; as far as the east is from the west, so far has He removed our transgressions from us. As a father pities his children, so the Lord pities those who fear Him.

■ PSALM 103:11-13

The Lord opens the eyes of the blind. The Lord lifts the burdens of those bent beneath their loads. The Lord loves the righteous.

■ PSALM 146:8 NLT

Here is another Old Testament verse that points to God's sheer delight in us. I bet you didn't know that He sings over you!

Did you know that you make Him so happy that He loves you, and He rejoices in the fact that you are who you are?

The Lord your God in your midst, the Mighty One, will save; He will rejoice over you with gladness, He will quiet you with His love, He will rejoice over you with singing.

■ ZEPHANIAH 3:17

The New Testament is also full of Scriptures that show God's unfailing love for us. This verse in John speaks of His feelings right before His crucifixion.

Just before the Passover Feast, Jesus knew that the time had come to leave this world to go to the Father. Having loved his dear companions, he continued to love them right to the end.

■ JOHN 13:1 MESSAGE

When Jesus left the earth after His resurrection, He showed His love for us again by not leaving us alone. He sent the Holy Spirit to dwell in our hearts to comfort and direct us.

And this expectation will not disappoint us. For we know how dearly God loves us, because he has given us the Holy Spirit to fill our hearts with his love.

■ ROMANS 5:5 NLT

The book of Romans is the foundational book for the Christian walk. Paul spells out so clearly the extent of God's love and protection for us in Romans 8:31-39.

What then shall we say to these things? If God is for us, who can be against us? He who did not spare His own Son, but delivered Him up for us all, how shall He not with Him also freely give us all things? Who shall bring a charge against God's elect? It is God who justifies. Who is he who condemns? It is Christ who died, and furthermore is also risen, who is even at the right hand of God, who also makes intercession for us. Who shall separate us from the love of Christ? Shall tribulation, or distress, or persecution, or famine, or nakedness, or peril, or sword? As it is written: "For Your sake we are killed all day long; we are accounted as sheep for the slaughter." Yet in all these things we are more than conquerors through Him who loved us. For I am persuaded that neither death nor life, nor angels nor principalities nor powers, nor things present nor things to come, nor height nor depth, nor any other created thing, shall be able to separate us from the love of God which is in Christ Jesus our Lord.

God's love didn't begin the moment you were born or even conceived. He knew you long before the foundations of the earth were laid. He planned a destiny especially for you, a destiny that only you could fulfill.

That destiny is designed to bring you more satisfaction and fulfillment than you could ever imagine, and just think, it gave Him so much pleasure planning it just for you!

How blessed is God! And what a blessing he is! He's the Father of our Master, Jesus Christ, and takes us to the high places of blessing in him. Long before he laid down earth's foundations, he had us in mind, had settled on us as the focus of his love, to be made whole and holy by his love. Long, long ago he decided to adopt us into his family through Jesus Christ. (What pleasure he took in planning this!) He wanted us to enter into the celebration of his lavish gift-giving by the hand of his beloved Son.

■ EPHESIANS 1:3-6 MESSAGE

Wow, and it gets even better! Ephesians 2 shows the state we were in when He chose to love us.

But God, who is rich in mercy, because of His great love with which He loved us, even when we were dead in trespasses, made us alive together with Christ (by grace you have been saved.)

■ EPHESIANS 2:4,5

Titus 3:4-5 makes it clear that it was out of His kindness and love that He chose to save us; we didn't do anything to earn salvation.

But when the kindness and the love of God our Savior toward man appeared, not by works of righteousness which we have done, but according to His mercy He saved us, through the washing of regeneration and renewing of the Holy Spirit.

Finally, First John shows us what real love is:

Anyone who does not love does not know God—for God is love. God showed how much he loved us by sending his only Son into the world so that we might have eternal life through him. This is real love. It is not that we loved God, but that he loved us and sent his Son as a sacrifice to take away our sins.

■ 1 JOHN 4:8-10 NLT

FORGIVENESS AND RESTORATION

You may think you've done something so bad that God can't forgive or love you. But God's mercy covers any sin you can imagine. You probably haven't broken all of the Ten Commandments, and even if you have, there is forgiveness available. King David is proof. He broke every single one of the Ten Commandments, yet God forgave him and restored him to fellowship. (2 Sam. 11,12; and Ps. 51.) David even earned the title "a man after God's own heart."

THE WORD OF GOD IS POWERFUL

The Bible confirms the power it contains by telling us in Hebrews 4:12 NLT:

The word of God is full of living power. It is sharper than the sharpest knife, cutting deep into our innermost thoughts and desires. It exposes us for what we really are.

That power can bring us victory in life. Reading, meditating on, and studying God's Word is the key to living a power-filled Christian life. The Word teaches us what sin is and how to avoid it. It gives you the power to conquer sin, and it shows you the power of God's forgiveness when you inevitably fail.

Through both scriptural principles and true stories of believers of the past, the Bible teaches us what it means to live the abundant life and how to do it. When we read and obey the

Word of God, we grow in our knowledge of Christ. The more we know Him, the more we will want to obey Him and His Word.

As human beings, our natural tendency is to think we know what we want or need, but the Bible can show us what's best for us. God doesn't want you to have what's "good" for you; He wants what's "best" for you. The Pharisees wanted the release of Barabbas, but who they really needed was Jesus. One of the key principles in the Bible is this: First and foremost, want Jesus, or you'll miss it.

> *"But seek first the kingdom of God and His righteousness, and all these things shall be added to you."*

> ■ MATTHEW 6:33

Notice it says "all these things." In the preceding verses, Jesus tells the crowd not to worry about food, shelter, or clothing, because God will provide these things. When you spend time in God's Word, you won't be needy. You won't have to look for artificial means of fulfillment; you'll find ultimate fulfillment in God. We're not to seek after the things, but instead we're to seek after God, and He will make sure we have everything we need.

PRAYER OF COMMITMENT TO SPENDING TIME IN GOD'S WORD

Father God, I commit to You right now, in the name of Jesus, to spend more time in Your Word. Your Word is my necessary food for daily living, and I choose to value and treasure it. Thank You for creating a desire in me for more of You. I thank You that if I hunger and thirst for righteousness, You have promised I will be filled. I thank You that You meet my every need as I commit to learning more about You from Your Word. Thank You for sealing this commitment in my heart, in Jesus' name. Amen. (Job 23:12; Matt. 5:6; Phil. 4:19; Ps. 37:4.)

BIBLE READING PLAN

IF YOU HAVE NEVER READ THROUGH THE BIBLE, I ENCOURAGE YOU TO DO SO. BY FOLLOWING THE PLAN I HAVE MAPPED OUT IN THE APPENDIX, YOU WILL BE ABLE TO READ THROUGH THE ENTIRE BIBLE IN ONE YEAR. IT BASICALLY WORKS LIKE THIS: SIX DAYS OF THE WEEK YOU READ TWO CHAPTERS IN THE OLD TESTAMENT AND ONE IN THE NEW TESTAMENT; THEN ON SUNDAY, READ THREE OLD TESTAMENT CHAPTERS AND TWO NEW TESTAMENT CHAPTERS. WHEN YOU FINISH THE NEW TESTAMENT, BEGIN READING PSALMS USING THE SAME PLAN.

There are many different Bible translations from which to choose. The two most important things to consider when selecting a translation for your daily reading are, 1) Is it a reputable, accurate translation? and 2) Can I understand it?

QUESTIONS FOR DISCUSSION AND REFLECTION

1. Define revival in your own words. What does that mean to you? What degree of revival are you experiencing in your life?

2. God's Word is the primary method He has chosen to teach you about His love. Do you have a problem with understanding God's love for you?

3. Read the Scriptures on God's love listed in this chapter. When you read them, make them personal by putting your name in the verse. For example: "For God so loved *Sarah* that He gave His only begotten Son so that if *I* believe in Him *I* can have eternal life." Write down your thoughts and feelings as your read each verse.

4. What functions is the Word of God intended to serve in your life? Are you taking advantage of all of the ways God wants to show Himself to You? How?

5. What are some of the things that cause your focus to shift off of God? What is God's perspective on those things?

6. Is there something that you want in life that you think may not line up with what God knows is best for you?

7. Is the Word of God a priority in your life? If not, what changes can you make in your daily routine to make it a priority?

8. What does Hebrews 4:12 use as a picture of God's Word? What does it expose?

9. In the following chapters, you will learn what you can do to keep revival alive in your heart. Before you read further, what do you think some of those things might be?

Chapter Two

Why Do I Need To Meditate on God's Word?

Meditation? Do you picture sitting on the floor in the lotus position "omming" and humming? That's not it at all! God's style of meditation is designed to engage the mind, rather than create an escape from it. God never meant for you to escape from life. He meant for you to fully engage in it, overcome obstacles, and live the victorious life that results from meditating on His Word.

God commanded Joshua to meditate on His Word, and He promised him that if he did, he would be successful. Joshua was a success in life. Later in this chapter, we'll look at the evidence of Joshua's success.

WHAT IS MEDITATION?

The kind of meditation the Bible speaks of is not Eastern-style meditation. It's not about disengaging the mind and letting it take you where it will. It's about engaging your mind and precisely focusing it on God's Word. There are many benefits to meditating.

You will notice after you have learned a verse that it continues to speak to you long after you move on to other verses. Meditating on God's Word is much like the process a cow uses in digesting her food. Cows have two stomachs. Initially, they chew their food and it goes into the first stomach to be digested so the nutrients can be absorbed. Then after a little bit, the cow regurgitates her digested food from the first stomach, chews on it some more, and then swallows it into the second stomach. (Yes, it sounds gross, but God made them that way for a reason. Maybe just to provide an illustration of how meditation works!) In the second stomach even more nutrients are squeezed out of the food. By the time the cow is finished with this digestion process, she has absorbed as many nutrients as she possibly can from her food.

When you meditate on the Word of God, you take it into your mind. As you memorize the verses and meditate on them, you gain certain insights. When you go on to other things, your subconscious mind is still "chewing" on the verses. When you go back to your verses for further study and meditation, you bring them back to your mind (or "regurgitate" them) and gain even more insight. You begin to remember more of the verses each time. You've squeezed out the nutrients. Eventually, the verses are "swallowed" into your heart and become a part of you. "You are what you eat." Those Scriptures will continue to speak to you long after you've moved on to meditate on and memorize other verses.

Psalm 119 tells us some of the benefits of meditating on God's Word:

How can a young person stay pure?
By obeying your word and following its rules.

■ PSALM 119:9 NLT

Your word I have hidden in my heart,
that I might not sin against You.

■ PSALM 119:11

MAKE A COMMITMENT

Revelation results from resolution and responsibility. When you make a commitment to meditate on God's Word and carry out your commitment, you will bear fruit in your life and it will help you know God more intimately. I know this is true because of God's promise in Isaiah 55:10-11:

"For as the rain comes down, and the snow from heaven, and do not return there, but water the earth, and make it bring forth and bud, that it may give seed to the sower and bread to the eater, so shall My word be that goes forth from my mouth; it shall not return to Me void, but it shall accomplish what I please, and it shall prosper in the thing for which I sent it."

JOSHUA'S SUCCESS

When Joshua took over as the leader of Israel, God commanded him to meditate on His Word. He said:

"This Book of the Law shall not depart from your mouth, but you shall meditate in it day and night, that you may observe to do according to all that is written in it. For then you will make your way prosperous, and then you will have good success."

■ JOSHUA 1:8

21

In this verse, God tells Joshua that the key to being successful and prosperous is meditating on His Word and putting it into practice. Joshua believed God's promise was true, and he lived by that principle. As you'll see, his life is proof of this promise.

When God gave Joshua this command, he was eighty years old, and Moses, the man who had been his leader for forty years, was dead. In the natural, it didn't look like Joshua had the potential for the success God described. He was an old man, and the man he had faithfully followed and loyally served for forty years was dead. Joshua was feeling lost. Moses was his mentor, and now he was gone.

This was the same Moses who split the Red Sea. The same Moses who unleashed the ten plagues on Egypt. The same Moses who led the Israelites in the desert for forty years. The same Moses to whom God gave the Ten Commandments on Mount Sinai. The same Moses who built the tabernacle. Joshua had big shoes to fill!

He had been taught for forty years how to lead people in the desert, not how to go in and conquer a country. It's no wonder God said to him over and over, "Be strong and of good courage." Before God told Joshua to be strong, however, He told him that the key to realizing his destiny was to meditate on the Word.

God said, "If you meditate on My Word, you will be prosperous and successful in everything you do." In the book of Joshua, we can see the evidence of his success. He put this principle of meditating on God's Word into practice and lived a successful, prosperous life. Let's look at four areas of Joshua's life—his family, his achievements, his finances, and his health—and witness his success.

NUMBER 1: FAMILY

At the end of Joshua's life, what was the condition of his family? In Joshua 24:15, Joshua proclaims:

"And if it seems evil to you to serve the Lord, choose for yourselves this day whom you will serve, whether the gods which your fathers served that were on the other side of the River, or the gods of the Amorites, in whose land you dwell. But as for me and my house, we will serve the Lord."

Joshua's entire family served God. That was pretty amazing. So Joshua was obviously successful in his family.

NUMBER 2: ACHIEVEMENTS

So Joshua took all this land: the mountain country, all the South, all the land of Goshen, the lowland, and the Jordan plain—the mountains of Israel and its lowlands, from Mount Halak and the ascent to Seir, even as far as Baal Gad in the Valley of Lebanon below Mount Hermon. He captured all their kings, and struck them down and killed them. Joshua made war a long time with all those kings.

■ JOSHUA 11:16-18

In seven years Joshua and his army conquered all of the Promised Land and defeated thirty-one armies. (Josh. 12:7-24.) Remember, Joshua's army didn't have tanks or helicopters or even guns. They had spears, sticks, rocks, and bows and arrows.

In one amazing battle, Joshua commanded the sun and moon to stand still until his army had the victory. The earth stopped spinning. It stayed suspended in time, while they continued to fight and win the battle.

> Then Joshua spoke to the Lord in the day when the Lord deliv-
> ered up the Amorites before the children of Israel, and he said in
> the sight of Israel: "Sun, stand still over Gibeon; and Moon, in
> the Valley of Aijalon." So the sun stood still, and the moon
> stopped, till the people had revenge upon their enemies. Is this
> not written in the Book of Jasher? So the sun stood still in the
> midst of heaven, and did not hasten to go down for about a
> whole day. And there has been no day like that, before it or after
> it, that the Lord heeded the voice of a man; for the Lord fought
> for Israel.

> ■ JOSHUA 10:12-14

In Joshua 24:31 we see what I consider Joshua's most significant achievement.

> Israel served the Lord all the days of Joshua, and all the days of
> the elders who outlived Joshua, who had known all the works of
> the Lord which He had done for Israel.

Throughout Joshua's lifetime, Israel served the Lord. They wouldn't do that even under Moses. They were fickle. They com-
plained incessantly. They wanted to go back to Egypt. When Moses went up on Mount Sinai to get the Ten Commandments, the Israelites were down below having a wild party and making a golden calf to worship. Joshua took the descendants of this group

of inconsistent gripers and complainers and turned them into a people who faithfully served the Lord. Because of Joshua's strong leadership, Israel continued to serve God under the elders even after he died.

Number 3: Finances

God prospered Joshua tremendously throughout his life. When he went into the Promised Land and conquered it, at the end of his work he was given the mountain of Timnath Serah.

According to the word of the Lord they gave him the city which he asked for, Timnath Serah in the mountains of Ephraim; and he built the city and dwelt in it.

■ Joshua 19:50

Joshua owned an entire mountain with a city on top. In Denver, you would be considered extremely wealthy if you owned an entire mountain, let alone one with a city on top. God's rewards to those who obey Him are tremendous.

Number 4: Health

People say that all the money in the world can't buy your health back. True prosperity includes living in health.

We find the evidence of Joshua's health and long life in Joshua 24:29.

Now it came to pass after these things that Joshua the son of Nun, the servant of the Lord, died, being one hundred and ten years old.

Joshua lived to be one hundred and ten years old. My grandma suffered greatly the last two years of her life. I wouldn't wish that kind of suffering on my worst enemy. But that's not the way Joshua died. He was not weak at the end of his one hundred and ten years; he lived a vibrant life. He was still strong. He was strong and courageous and then he died.

We can see from these four areas, Joshua had a very success-ful, prosperous life. True prosperity includes all four of these areas: achievement, family, wealth, and health. The key to his success in every area was meditating on the Word. Sometimes we come up with every excuse of why we can't meditate. But the bottom line is, when we don't meditate on the Word, we miss the success and prosperity God has for us. God will take care of you if you seek Him first. Look at Matthew 6:33 again, from *The Message:*

Steep your life in God-reality, God-initiative, God-provisions. Don't worry about missing out. You'll find all your everyday human concerns will be met.

THREE STEPS IN MEDITATION

There are three helpful steps in meditation. These steps will help you get the most out of the verses on which you are meditating.

Step 1: Memorization

The first step in meditation is memorization. Man has used memorization for centuries. Until fairly recently, man had to use his memory to retain most stories, poems, and songs. Early Greek and Roman orators had to commit their long speeches to memory. We have the Old Testament today because Jewish men memorized all of it and passed it down to their sons who learned it and passed it on. It was important to them to keep it accurate in their minds because it was the history of God interacting with their forefathers.

In Jesus' day, memorizing the Word was an important part of a young boy's education. By the time he was twelve, a Hebrew youth could quote much of the Pentateuch (the first five books of the Bible) from memory. By the time Jesus entered His ministry, many believe He had memorized most of the Old Testament.

Don't let the word *memorization* make you nervous. God knows the difficulties we face when we attempt to memorize His Word. Therefore, He has instructed the Holy Spirit to help us remember. Jesus says in John 14:26 NLT:

When the Father sends the Counselor as my representative— and by the Counselor I mean the Holy Spirit—he will teach you everything and will remind you of everything I myself have told you.

Before you start to memorize, ask God to help you, and the Holy Spirit will help you remember the verses you are studying. Then be responsive to the Spirit's prompting. If you sense your

---

need to review some verses, then do it! God is tugging at your heart in His own gentle way.

One of my friends started memorizing Scripture when she was first saved and had no Christian training. Memorizing helped introduce her to God. Since she knew nothing about the Bible or Christianity, her mind was a blank slate on which God could write who He is and what He does. It cleansed her mind from the past and centered it on what God says, what it means to be saved, and who we are in Christ.

Another friend told me about her son and how he was having problems in school. He had been diagnosed with Attention Deficit Disorder (ADD) and was having some rather serious difficulties related not only to his behavior, but also to his grades. His mom and he agreed that he should try to do some memorizing from the Bible, and so he began to work on the book of Proverbs a little bit at a time. By the end of the semester, his grades had gone up from very low C's to low A's and high B's. Both the mother and the son attributed this improvement to his memorizing the book of Proverbs.

MEMORY TIPS

- Write the verses on "stickies" and put them in places where you'll see them often (the bathroom mirror, in your car, on your computer monitor, etc.).
- Practice reciting the verses to the rhythm of your walking or exercising.

- Write the verses on cards and keep them in the restroom, so you can look at them when you're "resting."

- Review the verses at lunch and on breaks.

- First thing in the morning, read the verses out loud several times.

- Write the verses out several times.

- Begin memorizing a new verse the last thing before going to bed each night.

Step 2: Personalization

The second step in meditation is personalization. Personalizing the verses you mediate on is an invaluable tool. Think about how the Scripture applies to your life. How does it change you, comfort you, or challenge you? Make it personal; apply it to yourself and your situations.

One of my friends once confided he was having a very difficult time memorizing but had overcome his frustration by picturing himself in the verses being memorized. Not only can you put yourself into the events that are being described or discussed in the verses, you can also replace the nouns, "I, me, my," etc. with your name.

For example, if I were meditating on 2 Corinthians 5:17 KJV, I would read it like this:

Therefore, if [Sarah] *be in Christ,* [Sarah] *is a new creature; old things are passed away; behold, all things are become new.*

As we personalize God's Word, it becomes alive and active in our hearts. Personalizing it helps us to see its relevance in our lives. Then the Word is able to change us and shape us into God's image as we yield to it. Ask the Holy Spirit to make the Word you are memorizing personal and applicable to you. Put yourself in the verses, savoring them as descriptions of who you are.

Step 3: Visualization

The third step to meditation is visualization. God often uses word pictures to illustrate spiritual principles. When we visualize those word pictures, God's Word comes alive for us. The book of Proverbs is full of word pictures. For example, in Proverbs 1, wisdom is pictured as a woman calling out in the streets, searching high and low for someone who will value her words.

Another example is in the book of the prophet Ezekiel. In chapter 37, God uses the picture of a valley of dry bones coming to life to illustrate to Ezekiel how He was going to bring Israel back to life.

> *"Thus says the Lord God to these bones: 'Surely I will cause breath to enter into you, and you shall live. I will put sinews on you and bring flesh upon you, cover you with skin and put breath in you; and you shall live. Then you shall know that I am the Lord.'"*

■ EZEKIEL 37:5,6

You can just picture the bones rising up and the tendons and muscles growing and attaching the bones together. Then the skin grows and covers everything. If you've ever seen a demonstration of how animators use computers to build lifelike characters, you can easily envision this scene. The process animators use matches God's description here. They build the skeleton, then cover it with muscle, and then they put the skin on.

In verse 9, God tells Ezekiel to command the four winds to breathe life into the newly flesh-covered bones. You can close your eyes and picture an army of lifeless bodies. Picture the breeze coming up, gently at first, and their hair begins to ruffle—the first signs of life. Then as the wind gets stronger, it comes from every direction and you can see their stomachs expand as the breath of life is blown into their lungs. That's a pretty vivid picture, isn't it? Read Ezekiel 37:1-14 to get the whole picture. You will most likely never forget it. (Which would make it a great passage to memorize!)

Jesus taught by using nature to visually portray the kingdom of heaven. In Matthew 5:13-16, Jesus describes believers as "the salt of the earth" and "the light of the world." In chapter 7, he tells the story of two men who built a house. The wise man, the one who hears Jesus' words and obeys them, is like a man who builds his house on a rock. The foolish man's house is built on sand. Look at what Jesus says will happen to that man's house.

And the rain descended, the floods came, and the winds blew and beat on that house; and it fell. And great was its fall.

■ MATTHEW 7:27

Our society is very visual. We tend to remember things better when we see them or when we use our imagination to create vivid situations and pictures in which we are personally involved, but not all Scriptures lend themselves so readily to visualization. Sometimes you have to be a little more creative and use your imagination.

For example, if I were meditating on First John 1:9, "If we confess our sins, He is faithful and just to forgive us our sins and to cleanse us from all unrighteousness," I would picture my ever-faithful and just friend, Jesus, telling me from the cross that He has forgiven me. Then, I would picture myself writing my sins on a giant chalkboard. Jesus would walk up with a garden hose and wash them all away.

Since not all Scripture lends itself so obviously to visualization, get creative. Use these tips to help you picture the verses.

VISUALIZATION TIPS

1. ADD MOTION.

2. THE MORE UNUSUAL THE PICTURE, THE MORE MEMORABLE IT WILL BE.

3. USE UNUSUAL COMBINATIONS. (USE ANIMALS TO HELP YOU REMEMBER NAMES IN DIFFICULT PASSAGES, SUCH AS BASHAN/BULLS, PHILIPPIANS/PELICAN.)

KEEPING REVIVAL ALIVE

One of the main keys to keeping revival alive in your heart is to continually saturate your heart and life with the Word through meditation and memorization. Meditation also helps you to overcome sin. Romans 3:23 tell us, "All have sinned and fall short of the glory of God." And John tells us that no one is basically a "good person."

If we say that we have not sinned, we make Him a liar, and His word is not in us.

■ 1 JOHN 1:10

SCRIPTURES TO MEDITATE ON TO OVERCOME SPECIFIC SINS:

Malicious Thoughts
Philippians 4:8,9
Psalm 139:1,2
Matthew 15:16-20
Hebrews 3:1
Hebrews 4:12,13
2 Corinthians 10:5

Cheating/Stealing
Psalm 62:10-12
Proverbs 6
Leviticus 19:11
Ephesians 4:28
1 Corinthians 6:7-11

Selfishness
Philippians 2:3,4
Galatians 5:18-21
1 John 4:11
1 Peter 4:8,9
Galatians 5:13,14
Romans 12:10

Lack of Self-Control
1 Corinthians 9:24-27
Galatians 5:22-25
Titus 1:7-9
2 Peter 1:3-8

Thoughts of Revenge
Hebrews 10:30
1 Thessalonians 5:15
James 4:11
Romans 12:17-19

Lying
Psalm 25:21
Proverbs 10:9
Psalm 119:28-32
Proverbs 12:22
Ephesians 4:22-25
Colossians 3:9,10

Disrespect to Authority
Philippians 2:5-11
1 Peter 5:5
Romans 13:1-4

1 Timothy 2:1-4
Jude 5-9
1 Peter 2:13-17

Ungodly Anger
Proverbs 14:29
Proverbs 16:32
James 1:19,20
Colossians 3:8
Psalm 37:8

Gossip
Ephesians 4:31
1 Thessalonians 4:11,12
Colossians 4:6
Psalm 15:1-3
Psalm 34:13
James 1:26

Lust
Proverbs 6
Proverbs 11:6
Galatians 5:16,17
Matthew 5:27,28
1 Thessalonians 4:3-7
1 John 2:15-17

Unforgiveness
Matthew 6:14
Matthew 5:44,45
Mark 11:25
Luke 6:35,36
Colossians 3:12-14
Ephesians 4:32

However, meditation on God's Word will keep revival burning in your heart and cause you to be successful in every area of your life. It is important to remember that effective meditation requires daily practice. If you have consistently hidden God's Word in your heart, the book of Proverbs promises:

Wherever you walk, their counsel can lead you. When you sleep, they will protect you. When you wake up in the morning, they will advise you.

■ PROVERBS 6:22 NLT

PRACTICE MAKES PERFECT

The way in which you practice is one of the keys to success. In any sports activity, a good coach will watch his players practice, making sure they execute the fundamentals correctly. When I was growing up, I loved to play basketball. I would go out and practice for two to three hours a day, which was very helpful. However, when I shot the ball, I would shoot from my hip because I was too weak to shoot over my head. I had poor form, and I continued to practice using this poor shooting form. The erroneous way that I continued to shoot developed into a bad habit. As a result of my poor shooting form, it was easy for anyone to block the ball.

My junior high school coach really tried to help me. Every time I shot the ball wrong, it reinforced my bad habit, which made me a less effective player. So my coach would constantly remind me in practice to change my shooting form. My bad habit was hard to break because I had practiced improperly for such a long time. However, whenever I shot the ball correctly, it helped develop my muscles so that I could eventually shoot well. The more I progressed and developed in my basketball skills, the more important it was for me to use proper form.

When we exercise our spiritual muscles properly, we gain benefits that will last a lifetime. The apostle Paul admonished Timothy:

Exercise daily in God—no spiritual flabbiness, please! Workouts in the gymnasium are useful, but a disciplined life in God is far more so, making you fit both today and forever.

■ I TIMOTHY 4:8 MESSAGE

The way in which we practice Christianity, and meditation in particular, will give us a glimpse into our future success and effectiveness as a Christian. Therefore, as we learn to meditate on God's Word by memorizing, personalizing, and visualizing, we have the potential to experience the same kind of success and prosperity that Joshua experienced.

PRAYER OF COMMITMENT TO MEDITATING ON GOD'S WORD

Father God, I commit my mind to You. I pray that You would help me to keep You first in my life. Thank You for the Holy Spirit who walks alongside of me and reminds me of Your words. I thank You that You have given me the mind of Christ. I pray that my mind will be renewed to Your way of thinking as I meditate on Your Word. Help me to focus my thoughts and gain Your wisdom, so that I can live a successful prosperous life like Joshua. In Jesus' name, amen. (John 14:26; 1 Cor. 2:16; Rom. 12:2; 2 Cor. 10:5.)

SUGGESTED PASSAGES TO MEMORIZE AND MEDITATE ON

Ephesians 6:11-18—Putting on the Full Armor of God

Psalm 27—The Lord Is our Stronghold and Shelter

Psalm 91—God Is our Protector

Matthew 5:1-16—Jesus' Sermon on the Mount

1 Corinthians 13—The Love Chapter

Proverbs 31:10-31—The Virtuous Woman

Psalm 63—Earnestly Seeking After God

Psalm 103—Praising God

John 15:1-17—Abiding in Christ

Hebrews 11:3-40—Heroes of the Faith

QUESTIONS FOR DISCUSSION AND REFLECTION

1. How is the meditation the Bible speaks of different from Eastern-style meditation?

2. What are some of the benefits of meditating on God's Word? What is the process of meditation? (Not the three steps, but the process as illustrated by a cow chewing her cud.)

3. What did God command Joshua to do in order to have a successful, prosperous life? Was Joshua a success in life? How so?

4. What are three things you can do that will aid you in meditating on God's Word?

5. What did Jesus promise you in John 14:26 that will aid you in memorizing God's Word? Have you ever experienced that in this or any area? What happened?

6. How can you apply the benefits of meditating on God's Word to your daily life? And what steps can you take to make meditation an effective part of your daily life?

7. Look at the verses listed on the chart on pages 34-35. Is there a sin listed with which you personally struggle? Look up the verses listed under that heading and pick the one that ministers to you. Write it out below, personalizing it by putting your name in it.

8. I used my experience in practicing basketball to make a point about how important "proper" practice is. Can you think of an example from your own life where this principle has been true?

Chapter Three
How Can I Hear God's Voice?

God is constantly speaking to us, but the distractions of our modern lives often prohibit us from hearing Him. We must learn how to actively listen and be attentive to the many ways He speaks. The number one way God speaks to us is through his written Word, but he also speaks to us through conversations, relationships, repetition, and circumstances. I'll cover each of these areas in depth throughout this chapter. Often, all that's necessary for you to hear God speaking is to step out of the fast lane, if only for a moment.

LIFE IS FULL OF DISTRACTIONS

There are so many things vying for our attention, we don't even realize it—TV, billboards, radio, work, home, family. There is a constant pulling this way, pulling that way, pulling every which way.

Think of the Internet. There are so many different buttons and links and banners to click on. You can go a hundred different directions (and sometimes more!) from a single page. There are ads flashing at you and popping up on your screen. Somebody always wants your attention.

However, the person who most wants your attention is your loving Father God. He wants to communicate with you, give you direction, encourage you, and more. But all of these outside things pull, pull, pull, and you only have so much capacity. You get so distracted; you lose sight of how God speaks to you. Your mind is filled with so many competing voices that God's still, small voice is drowned out. Sometimes we think He's not speaking any more, but He is and we're just not aware of it. I believe that's why God speaks in a "still, small voice" on the inside, so that you have to slow down and quiet your mind to listen. If you didn't have to slow down, you would miss the opportunity to be refreshed.

Often, when we do manage to slow down and get quiet for a while, we struggle with discerning God's voice. We think, *Is this the devil? Is this just my brain? Or is this really God?*

GOD DOES SPEAK

There are many different ways God speaks to us, and if we're aware of them, we'll see that He's speaking to us constantly. In the book of Job, after he has complained that God has been silent, Job's friend Elihu says:

God speaks again and again, though people do not recognize it. He speaks in dreams, in visions of the night when deep sleep falls on people as they lie in bed. He whispers in their ear and terrifies them with his warning. He causes them to change their minds; he keeps them from pride.

■ JOB 33:14-17 NLT

Now look again at verse 14. It says, "For God does speak, now one way now another, though man may not perceive it." God is always speaking to us one way or another, but sometimes we tune Him out. We don't catch what He's saying. We think, *God, why don't You speak where I can hear You?* But God is trying to broaden your ability to hear Him. He's trying to give you greater understanding. We're just too narrow-minded in our thinking sometimes.

We say, "No, God, You've got to speak to me in this context. Just through the Bible."

But God is saying, *No. I want to talk to you in this way and that way and in another way. I want to speak to you in a multitude of ways so that you get to know Me better.* We limit how we hear God by our narrow frame of reference. God is multidimensional. He wants to be involved with us on every level of our lives, not just according to our limited understanding of Him.

God doesn't always use words to speak to us. The Hebrew word for "speak" in Job 33:14 actually deals with events or situations.[1] Sometimes God speaks to us through circumstances, rather than in words. We wish He would write it on the wall like He did in the book of Daniel, but that only happened once in Scripture and it wasn't exactly a positive message. (See Dan. 5:17-31.)

"For God does speak…though man may not perceive it."

■ JOB 33:14

The word *perceive* in Hebrew means "to spy out, to survey."[2] Sometimes when I have a conversation with my husband, I just don't listen very well. I'm not very attentive. I don't "perceive" what he's saying. I may hear him with my ears, but its not registering in my brain.

When I was a teacher, I had this problem with my students. They would just zone out. Their bodies were there, but their minds were long gone. We often do the same to God. He's speaking, but we're just not aware of it. We're not spying it out. We're not attentive. We don't perceive it.

When I was growing up and my parents traveled, I would stay with a friend's family. The mom had a very high-pitched little voice, and like many women, she loved to talk. I would notice from time to time that her husband would just suddenly "click" and tune out. They even joked about it at the dinner table. He called it "wife deafness."

In the same way (although God's voice is much more pleasant to listen to), God is trying to talk to us, but sometimes we just— "click"—tune out. He is always talking, though we may not grasp it because we've tuned out. The body is there, but the mind is long gone. Another Scripture that confirms God is speaking to us is Exodus 15:26:

> *"If you diligently heed the voice of the Lord your God and do what is right in His sight, give ear to His commandments and keep all His statutes, I will put none of the diseases on you which I have brought on the Egyptians. For I am the Lord who heals you."*

FINDING A QUIET SPACE TO HEAR FROM GOD

- Turn everything off—radio, TV, computer...

- Find a quiet spot—your favorite chair, in the car, under a tree...

- Take a notebook or journal with you, and write down any worries or cares that are distracting you; then put them out of your mind.

- Cast your cares on the Lord, and ask Him to quiet your mind. (Ps. 55:22.)

- Make an effort to listen quietly, focusing your attention on God.

- Write down the things God speaks to you.

Notice, He said, "If you diligently heed My voice." You can't "diligently heed" His voice if He's not talking, so He must be talking, right? Another translation says, "If you listen carefully." In the Hebrew, the word *listen* means "to hear with intelligence."[3] Some people say there is a difference between hearing and listening. When you "hear" something, it goes in one ear and out the other, but when you're actively listening, you process the information, you make sense of it, and you retain it. You can truly communicate with someone because you have heard them "with intelligence."

The next part of the verse tells us to "give ear [pay attention] to His commands." The Hebrew words for *pay attention* give the picture of broadening or opening up the ear so one can hear clearly,[4] such as the ear trumpets people used in the early 1900s.

An ear trumpet is a device that curves around like a snail, but it has a small end that goes in the ear and a large end that looks like the horn of a trumpet. People who were hard of hearing would hold the ear trumpet up to their ear, and it helped them to hear. It was the predecessor to the hearing aid. It made the ear "big" so they could hear. That's what *pay attention* means: to broaden the ear.

God wants to broaden our ears. He wants to broaden our ability to hear Him. He loves us and desires for us to know Him better, but we can only know Him better if we choose to listen to Him. God, the Creator of the universe, loves you and wants to talk to you in many ways!

There are different types of communication, both verbal and non-verbal. When you know someone really well—such as your best friend, spouse, or family members—you know what they're thinking or feeling even when they're not speaking out loud to you.

FIVE WAYS GOD SPEAKS TO YOU

There are five major ways God speaks to you.

Number 1: The first way God speaks to you is through His Word, the Bible.

When you spend time in His Word, you will learn to recognize His voice. If you're not spending time reading and studying your Bible, you probably won't recognize it when God speaks to you.

Sometimes we're in a church service and the minister will call people out and give them a Scripture. Usually the rest of us think, *Why doesn't somebody give me a Scripture?* My mom always says,

"You've got the whole Bible. Go check it out for yourself and see what God tells you." We want the minister to tell us what God's saying, but the minister can't be there with us day in and day out to be our translator. We need to be in the Bible every day for ourselves so we can recognize God's voice.

I know my husband very well. When he calls me, I recognize his voice. Why? Because I live with the guy. He talks to me all the time. We have good conversations. We have a good relationship. I don't even have to see him; I just know his voice when I hear it.

If we familiarize ourselves with the Word by spending time in it, we will recognize God's voice when we hear it. If what you're hearing is inconsistent with God's Word, then you'll know it's not God talking. There have been times in my life when I thought I heard God and I missed it. But if we saturate our minds with God's Word, we won't have to wonder if we're hearing from God, or if it's the devil or just our own mind.

Most of the time we don't have too much trouble telling the difference between God's voice and the devil's, but he can be very deceptive, so we've got to know the Word and know it well. The devil can use the Word to trick us. He even tried it with Jesus.

When Jesus was tempted in the wilderness, Satan said:

"If You are the Son of God, throw Yourself down from here. For it is written: 'He shall give His angels charge over You, to keep You,' and, 'In their hands they shall bear you up, lest you dash your foot against a stone.'"

■ LUKE 4:9-11

47

But Jesus knew the Word well enough to recognize the devil was twisting it. He was taking it out of context and manipulating it to tempt Jesus.

So Jesus replied, "It has been said, 'You shall not tempt the Lord your God'" (Luke 4:12).

If you know the Word well, then Satan won't be able to deceive you.

The difference between your own voice and God's voice can be the hardest to discern. If you've been in the Word, you'll know, because you'll know His voice. When you know the Word, you can use the following checkpoints to help you differentiate between these voices.

CHECKPOINTS TO DETERMINE IF YOU'RE HEARING GOD'S VOICE, SATAN'S VOICE, OR YOUR OWN

1. DOES IT LINE UP WITH THE WORD OF GOD?

2. DOES IT BEAR WITNESS IN YOUR HEART?

3. DO THE CIRCUMSTANCES LINE UP?

First, does it line up with the Word of God?

When I was twenty-four, I felt like God was telling me to go to China for the summer on a mission trip. God told me this in

January, so I thought, *Well, God, if that's really You we'll see. But I don't know. Is this me, the devil, or is it You, God?*

Well, did it line up with God's Word for me to go and minister in China? Yes, I believe it did. The Great Commission tells us to go into all the world and preach the gospel.

Second, does it bear witness in your heart?

This one can be tricky, but you know when you hear something if it lines up with the desires of your heart. You can't base it all on this one point; you have to use all three.

Sometimes we think we've heard from God and it bears witness in our heart, but we don't stop to see if it lines up with these other checkpoints, so we jump up and do something God didn't intend for us to do. Sometimes we get that inner witness and make a hasty decision. The best thing you can do sometimes is wait. God will bring it back to you when it's the proper time. You're not being disobedient; you're just making sure you heard God clearly and waiting for His timing.

Third, do the circumstances line up?

Again, you can't use this point alone to make a decision. Sometimes God tells us to do something, and our circumstances dictate exactly the opposite. But that's the exception, not the rule. When I felt I was to go to China, I checked it against the Word and it lined up. So I checked the inward witness and I had peace in my heart. Now, what about my circumstances?

Well at the time I was teaching in a Christian high school. Unfortunately, most Christian schools aren't able to pay their teachers a great deal of money. I was living with my parents and paying rent, but my car was paid for and everything was fine. But did I have the extra money for a trip to China? No, I didn't. So I prayed, "Father God, I know it's in agreement with Your Word for me to go to China and I have peace in my heart about going, so I'm asking You to cause my circumstances to line up."

By the end of February, God had worked a complete miracle. I had all the finances I needed to go to China and more. God had given me my answer. The circumstances were lined up.

Number 2: God speaks to us through our conversations.

When the disciples were walking along the road to Emmaus, someone came alongside them.

> *Now behold, two of them were traveling that same day to a village called Emmaus, which was about seven miles from Jerusalem. And they talked together of all these things which had happened. So it was, while they conversed and reasoned, that Jesus Himself drew near and went with them. But their eyes were restrained, so that they did not know Him.*
>
> ■ LUKE 24:13-16

They had no idea that it was Jesus walking with them. Finally, when they stopped to eat, Jesus broke the bread, and suddenly their eyes were opened and they recognized Him. But notice what they said:

> *"Did not our heart burn within us while He talked with us on the road, and while He opened the Scriptures to us?"*
>
> ■ LUKE 24:32

There are times when you'll have a conversation with some-one, and something they say will ring in your heart. It will keep coming back to you over and over. Let me give you a personal example. When I was teaching high school, I got really close to my students. I loved them all. Most of them are in college now, so when they come home for the summer, I like to have them over so I can see how they're progressing in their lives.

One evening we had about twenty-three of them at our home, and we started going around the room having everyone tell what had happened to them last semester at school. One boy was a student at Oral Roberts University, and he was talking about chapel. I was just kind of half paying attention because I was play-ing hostess and was busy with other things. But all of a sudden it was like I couldn't hear anything but him.

He said that a special speaker had been ministering in chapel, and one of the things he said was, "God can do through you what you cannot do." Well, when he said that, it was like somebody took a hot iron and seared that word in my heart. It was as if I were in a canyon, and that's all I heard for the next three or four minutes—echoing, echoing, echoing.

"God can do through you what you cannot do." It hit me like a ton of bricks. "God can do through you what you cannot do." It resounded inside me again and again and again.

I've also had it happen to me like this: Oftentimes I'll be sit-ting in church praying about the service and God will show me something from the Word, so I write it down. Then at the end of the service, when I'm having a conversation with someone, they'll say almost exactly the same thing to me. It resounds in my heart.

If you think about it, you may recall times when this has happened to you. Someone says something to you and it just burns in your heart. God seems to bring it back to you again and again.

Number 3: God speaks to you through relationships.

Each and every person in your life who loves you is an expression of God's love for you. Left to ourselves, human beings are not very loving. When you visit places like Auschwitz, Kosovo, Serbia, or Cambodia, you see that man is not inherently good. The goodness in our lives comes from God.

In our relationships we sometimes see the person but fail to recognize that God is loving us through them. I have a very loving father, I have a very loving husband, and I have a very loving mother. And in each of those people I perceive God's love for me in a different capacity. My dad loves me. I know that I'm the apple of his eye. I know he thinks I'm wonderful, and he knows me really well. But I take that as not only coming from my dad, but as an expression of my heavenly Father's love for me.

I love my dad; he is a really fun person. Nobody on the planet is like him. When I was growing up, I played basketball. My dad didn't like sports, so to come and watch junior high girls play basketball was pretty boring for him. It would be to just about anyone. So he would take his crossword puzzles and do them while I was playing basketball. I remember looking up thinking, *I wish he would watch the game.* But his way of expressing his love to me wasn't in that; it was different. He would watch out for me. He would protect me in different ways in order to express his love. Through his love, I learned to a small degree the love of my heavenly Father.

Maybe you had a poor relationship with your father. Maybe he was abusive or absent. Even in that case you can learn something about God. You can learn what He is not. You recognize that your earthly father is not the same as your heavenly Father. Your heavenly Father is the antithesis of your earthly father.

I know my husband loves me, and he knows I love him. I see his love as an expression from him, but I also see it as an expression of my heavenly Father's love.

My mom loves me. She's crazy about me. I know that. She shows it to me in a variety of ways. Even when she is correcting me, that's an expression that she loves me. She doesn't want me to stay the same. She wants me to grow. God desires for me to grow, so He is loving me through my mother.

My mom always told me that when I had children, I'd get a whole new perspective on God's love for me as His child, and that's true. If you have children, you can understand God's love in an even greater capacity through the love you have for your children.

If we see the people around us from that perspective—that God is loving us through them—it demonstrates to us the great love that God has for us. God communicates to us through our relationships.

Behold what manner of love the Father has bestowed on us, that we should be called children of God!

■ I JOHN 3:1

He expresses that love to you in a variety of ways. When someone does something for you, remember the heart behind it is

God telling you, "I love you. I love you. I love you." When you start to understand that, it will rock you. You will think, *Oh, I never knew God loved me to this degree!*

Number 4: God uses repetition to make His will known to you.

If you've ever taught a Bible study or been in any kind of teaching situation, you understand that one of the keys to learning is repetition. I think if God didn't repeat Himself, we'd probably miss 98 percent of what He says.

Jesus did this when He repeatedly healed on the Sabbath. He was trying to make a point to the Pharisees. He was saying, in essence, "I am Lord of the Sabbath." (Matt. 12:9-14; Mark 1:30,31; Luke 4:40; Luke 13:10-13; Luke 14:1-4.)

Sometimes God gets us from every side. Everywhere we go, we hear His message—through people we come across, on the radio, on TV. There have been times in my life when He has hammered me one time after another, after another, after another, after another, after another, after another, and finally I say, "Okay, I get it. I get it."

Recently God has been working on me in the area of friendship. I've been memorizing and meditating on First John. In chapters 3 and 4, it talks about loving people.

God has been helping me with this, but I'd been compartmentalizing it. I was limiting God's work in my life. But as I began to understand it, God brought some new people into my life. He said, *Here are some friends. You're going to like them.*

I said, "No I'm not."

Yes, you are.

Then He reminded me of First John 4. I realized that if I said I loved God but didn't love these people, then I had a problem. I wasn't being consistent and I wasn't really applying the Word in my life, so I submitted to God.

Later I was reading a book on an airplane and I "just happened" to come to a section on friendship. God was hitting me from every angle. Everything I was reading, everything I was meditating on, everything in my life was dealing with friendship.

I've also found this repetition to be extremely helpful in ministry. Oftentimes when I'm ministering and I sense God telling me to do something, I listen carefully and then wait. Sometimes I'm not sure if it's just me, or if it's God speaking, so I wait to see if God says it again. Usually, if I hear it again, I know it's God. Otherwise, my brain would be off onto something else. When I do that and I hear it again, it's been only a very rare occasion that I've missed it. You'll find that if you wait patiently for God to speak it again, He will.

Number 5: God speaks to us through various situations in our lives.

In John 8:3-11, we find the story of the woman caught in adultery. The Pharisees caught her in the act, and they dragged her out before Jesus.

> *"Teacher, this woman was caught in adultery, in the very act. Now Moses, in the law, commanded us that such should be stoned. But what do You say?"*

What does Jesus do? He doesn't answer their question directly; He starts to teach the people. He squats down and draws in the sand.

So when they continued asking Him, he raised Himself up and said to them, "He who is without sin among you, let him throw a stone at her first." And again He stooped down and wrote on the ground. Then those who heard it, being convicted by their conscience, went out one by one, beginning with the oldest even to the last.

And Jesus was left alone, and the woman standing in the midst. When Jesus had raised Himself up and saw no one but the woman, He said to her, "Woman, where are those accusers of yours? Has no one condemned you?" She said, "No one, Lord." And Jesus said to her, "Neither do I condemn you; go and sin no more."

Through that situation, Jesus taught the woman that He is not the accuser, but He is the forgiver.

I have experienced this many times in my own life. One time I was traveling, and in one week, I visited two different churches where the kids and in-laws were working under the parents. My husband, Reece, and I work in the church with my parents. We all have very strong personalities, and sometimes we all have different ideas about things. We all work together very well, but we are all unique. We each have different ideas, and they don't always mesh.

Visiting these churches was very encouraging to me because I witnessed two families in similar situations and it wasn't easy, but it was working. God was encouraging me through that life situation.

Not too long ago, there was a time in my life when I was very discouraged. I was having a hard time and was discouraged in the ministry. I was thinking, *I am going nowhere fast. This is the pits.* In the midst of that, I went to a church to minister. Before the service I was sitting in my hotel room, trying to prepare. But I was depressed and having a really hard time. I knew my depression and discouragement wasn't what people needed. It wasn't going to minister to or help anyone. They didn't need my discouragement they needed something from God. I asked God, "What do You want me to preach on?"

He answered, *I want you to preach on faith.*

Faith? I was depressed and discouraged, and God wanted me to minister on faith? So I went to the church service that night and preached on faith. I preached it hard, bold, and strong. I had nothing to lose; I was past the point of no return. No one knew that I was discouraged. I just thought, *Forget it. I've got nothing to lose.*

FIVE WAYS GOD SPEAKS TO YOU

NUMBER 1: THE FIRST WAY GOD SPEAKS TO YOU IS THROUGH HIS WORD, THE BIBLE.

NUMBER 2: GOD SPEAKS TO YOU THROUGH YOUR CONVERSATIONS.

NUMBER 3: GOD SPEAKS TO YOU THROUGH RELATIONSHIPS.

> NUMBER 4: GOD USES REPETITION TO MAKE HIS
> WILL KNOWN TO YOU.
>
> NUMBER 5: GOD SPEAKS TO YOU THROUGH
> VARIOUS SITUATIONS IN YOUR LIFE.

When I got back to my hotel room, I was crying. I was still so discouraged. The next morning when I woke up, I had to preach again. I asked God, "What do You want me to preach on?"

Faith.

"Oh no, not again."

So I preached on faith, and then I went back to my hotel and cried some more. Again, I was praying because I was going to have to speak one more time. "God, what do you want me to speak on?"

Faith.

"Not faith again! Give me a break. How can You have me preach on faith? Don't You know how I feel?"

And God said, *Exactly. You need to hear it for yourself.*

So I preached on faith again, and this time I let it change me. God used that situation and repetition in my life to encourage me and teach me something about trusting Him.

Another really good example of this is in Acts 17:26- 27. Paul is in Ephesus ministering and says:

"He has made from one blood every nation of men to dwell on all the face of the earth, and has determined the preappointed times and the boundaries of their dwellings, so that they should seek the Lord, in the hope that they might grope for Him and find Him, though He is not far from each one of us."

God has set up divine times, places, and events in your life for you to encounter Him, although He's not far from you. I'd like to couple that with the verse we used at the beginning of this chapter, Job 33:14.

For God may speak in one way, or in another, yet man does not perceive it.

God does speak in one way or another, although we don't always perceive it. He's setting up times, places, and events. At times you may not understand why certain things are happening, but God wants you to know He's broadening your capacity to hear Him. He's causing you to grow so you can hear from Him better and better.

I've seen this happen in relationships. When I first met my husband, I didn't like him at all. I was nineteen and I was going out to eat with some family friends. Reece was just tagging along. The relationship was between the pastor friends and me. But when we got to the restaurant and sat down, Reece started talking about politics. He talked the entire time. It was right after an election and he's really into politics, so he was fired up at the time. I know very little about politics, so I just wasn't interested.

Have you ever had that happen? What do you do? Most of us, either consciously or subconsciously, tune out. Your mind is off on other things. You're making your grocery list; you're thinking of all the errands you need to run, who you need to call, and so on. Meanwhile, you're saying all the right things to be polite, but really your mind is someplace else.

Sometimes we're like that with God. We talk and talk and talk and never give Him a chance to speak to us. We keep our praise and worship music going all the time. Or we keep the TV on all the time. Or we're at the computer all the time.

It's good to hear the Word and it's good to hear good music, but sometimes God wants to speak to you one on one. Turn off the radio. Turn off the TV. Close the books. Be still and listen. The Bible says, "Be still, and know that I am God" (Ps. 46:10). And Isaiah said:

But those who wait on the Lord will find new strength. They will fly high on wings like eagles. They will run and not grow weary. They will walk and not faint.

■ ISAIAH 40:31 NLT

There's nothing wrong with being still. I know as well as you do that it's very difficult to make your mind be still. Our thoughts bounce around like little rubber balls bouncing off the bathroom tile. Do you ever wrestle with that? I know I do. I tell God, "Father, help me. I'm tired of trying to chase my brain. Help me to be still. Help me to center. Help me to hear You." If you will pray that way, you'll be shocked at how quickly your mind will get still.

Another thing I've found that helps me to get quiet and focus is to write down the things that are bothering me. Then I tell myself, *I'll come back to that later, but for now I'm leaving it alone. I'm writing it down on this piece of paper, and I'll deal with it later. I need to listen to my heavenly Father right now.*

If you will make even the smallest effort to get quiet and be aware of the many opportunities God uses to speak to you, you'll realize that He is speaking to you all the time. And you'll notice it more and more. The most important thing to remember is that God loves you. He wants to talk to you. Just listen and be attentive; you'll hear Him.

PRAYER FOR EARS TO HEAR WHEN AND WHAT GOD IS SPEAKING

Heavenly Father, I pray that You would make my ears perceptive to Your speaking. Broaden my capacity to listen. Help me to clear the clutter and distractions from my life and my mind so I can hear what You are saying to me. I choose to be still and wait on You. Thank You for Your promise to speak to me. I choose to listen today and every day. In Jesus' name, amen.

QUESTIONS FOR DISCUSSION AND REFLECTION

1. Job 33:14 says God is always speaking. Why do you not always hear Him?

2. What does the Hebrew word for "speak" imply in Job 33:14? Does God always use words to speak to you?

3. What are some of the nonverbal ways God speaks to you?

4. What does it mean for us to "perceive" God speaking?

5. What does it mean to "diligently heed" God's voice?

6. How can you carve out more quiet time in your life to hear from God? What distractions can you eliminate from your life (or at least silence temporarily)?

7. Does God want to talk to you? Why?

8. Look at the five ways God speaks to you. Can you recall a time when He has used one or more of those means to speak to you?

9. What are some of the ways you can be sure you're hearing God's voice?

10. One of the ways God communicates His love to you is through relationships. Make a list of people in your life who love you. What does each of these people show you about God's love for you? Is there someone who shows you what God is not? Write down God's qualities that are the opposite of that person's.

Chapter Four

How Can I Encourage God To Speak to Me?

Radio, TV, Internet, E-mail, billboards, magazines! There are so many things that compete for our attention these days, and it only seems to get worse! We have to make a determined choice to step out of the fast lane and find a quiet spot where we can develop a quiet attitude and a heart that is ready to listen to God's voice. We must learn to be active listeners and eliminate competing voices (if only momentarily). We must be on the look-out for messages from God. They may come from very unexpected sources, but if we're paying attention, we will recognize them when they come our way.

I believe that you can encourage God to talk to you. You say, "What do you mean by that?" Well, I believe that you can do things that show God you value communication with Him. Think of this in relation to your mate, your children, or your best friend.

When I was a teenager, I would go out with my mom every Wednesday night. I loved having that time to spend with her. We'd go have a pizza and a salad. That was our relationship time.

We connected over that pizza and salad. Mom made it possible for me to communicate with her by being available. She set aside the time to listen to and communicate with me.

There are also things Mom did that helped pull that communication out. We sometimes do the opposite with God. We put up a brick wall and say, "No thanks. I don't want to hear from You today." We don't say it in so many words, but we say it with our actions, our behaviors. Likewise, there are things we can do to communicate to God, "Speak, Lord, for Your servant is listening."

For a brief time, I taught in an inner-city Sunday school class, but I was absolutely terrible. I was so bad they asked me not to come back. In my defense, I was used to more of a controlled environment. I taught high school. I was the teacher, the authority in the classroom, and I was in control. No problem. But when I taught in my inner-city Sunday school classroom, it wasn't the same.

I tried to communicate with the kids, and it was like talking to a brick wall. That was the attitude. We do the same thing to God.

Let's look at some of the things you can do to encourage God to speak to you. There are several things you can do, and they're really very simple.

Number 1: Listen.

That seems really simple, but you may not realize how often you're not listening. If you don't give God the chance to speak to you, then He stops talking. He doesn't do it out of spite or frustration; it is simply a matter of His waiting for an opportunity when you will listen.

Minimize the pull of the things that compete for your attention. The TV, the radio, the computer, the cell phone—all these things draw your attention away from God. I love all kinds of gadgets. I'm into computers. I'm into E-mail. I'm into surfing the Net. I like my CD player. I like the radio and my cell phone. I like all of that. All of that "stuff" competes for my attention.

Sometimes I feel as if God is saying, *Sarah, you're acting like you have Attention Deficient Disorder. You're all over the place. You're so focused over here, but I can barely get you to focus on Me.* If we will just listen, turn off the radio, turn off the TV, separate ourselves, and pull ourselves away from those distractions, we give God an opportunity to talk.

Now, I know we live in a very fast, very demanding world. I don't mean to deny that in any way. We may feel it's very difficult to slow down. There's never enough time in the day. On the other hand, however, we do have opportunities.

Church is often one of the few places where we focus on God long enough for Him to get through to us, but God will speak to us anywhere. We don't have to be in church on Sunday to hear from God. God wants to speak to us on Monday, Tuesday, Wednesday, Thursday, Friday, and Saturday—anywhere we are.

Case in point, I was having a conversation with a friend of mine one day, and he said, "I hear from God really well outside." When he is outside, away from other distractions, he can hear from God. If you run or walk, that's a great time to hear from God. Leave the CD or cassette player at home and just listen to Him.

Personally, in the past I'd hear from God very well when I was in my car. The radio didn't work, the tape player didn't work, and

I didn't have a CD player in it. So I could listen to the car running or I could focus on God. I have had some of the sweetest times of fellowship with God in my car while driving down the street. You might say, "But when I'm driving, I have to pay attention to the road." Well, of course you do, but you can find moments to listen to God if you want to. What about at the stoplights?

Just get quiet. Turn off the TV. Maybe before you go to bed. Perhaps you have a special room. Maybe it's in the bathroom! Give yourself an opportunity to listen. God will talk to you and you can talk to Him. Cultivate your ability to listen to God.

Number 2: Be attentive.

Be aware of what's going on in your life. Don't go through life at warp speed and miss what God is saying. Put your antennae out. Listen, watch, look, be attentive. Even if you have to step out of the fast lane for just a minute or two, reflect on what's going on in your life. Step off the fast track and say, "Wait a second. What's happening here?"

If you're attentive, you'll notice when God speaks to you, and then you may later run into someone who will tell you the exact same thing. If you're not paying attention, you'll miss those things.

This is an area where keeping a journal can be a tremendous help. Write down the things you feel God is speaking to you. Write down the things that are going on in your life. Write down the things people say to you that prick your heart. When you go back and review those things, you'll begin to see a pattern. God is trying to tell you something. Are you paying attention?

Number 3: Be Obedient.

Another thing that will help you hear from God is to be obedient. Sometimes God will tell you something and then wait for you to obey Him before He tells you the next thing. We keep saying, "Oh, God, talk to me." But He's already spoken. He told you what to do, and He's waiting for you to do it. Other times you may think that God is not talking to you, but He is; you just don't like what you're hearing.

If you have children, think about how you feel when they react to the things you say. If they obey you when you ask them to do something, it's easier for you to communicate with them than when they're constantly fighting you.

Pastor Cho in Korea has one of the biggest churches on the planet. More than 800,000 people attend his church. When someone asks him, "What's the secret to your success, Pastor Cho?" he says, "I pray and I obey." That's his secret. He prays and he obeys.

Charles Spurgeon said, "The world has yet to see what God can do through a man totally yielded to Him."

It's easy for us to be yielded on Sunday. We're all very compliant and obedient. Praise and worship is great, the message is great, the fellowship is great. It's easy to be obedient in church.

But what happens on Monday morning? What happens when everything's not going right? What happens when somebody cuts you off on the highway? That's when obedience counts.

Number 4: Be grateful.

When God speaks to you, be grateful. Say, "God, thank You for speaking to me. I appreciate that. I need Your love and encouragement. Thank You."

When we're grateful for the things people do for us, they want to bless us more. Think about your own children. When they say thank you, it means a lot. It makes you want to give them more.

The Bible declares:

Oh, give thanks to the Lord, for He is good! For His mercy endures forever.

■ I CHRONICLES 16:34

Paul prayed for the saints at Colossi:

May you be filled with joy, always thanking the Father, who has enabled you to share the inheritance that belongs to God's holy people, who live in the light.

■ COLOSSIANS 1:11,12 NLT

I believe our society is becoming less and less grateful. We often don't say thank you. When I was growing up, my mom taught me to always send a thank-you note. Why? Because it is good manners to do so. Express your appreciation to God when He speaks. You'll hear from Him more often.

Number 5: Treasure God's words.

When God speaks to you, write it down. There may be times when you think He's not speaking and you'll need that treasure trove of words from God to turn back to. Treasure His words; they're precious. Don't take them for granted. If you don't treasure and esteem His Word, why would He keep talking to you?

Think of your relationship with your spouse or a close friend. If you're talking to that person and they're not listening, do you want to keep talking to them?

We need to approach God the way Darth Vader approached the emperor in one of the *Star Wars* movies. He knelt before the emperor and said, "What is my master's bidding?" He wasn't asking for anything but his master's will. He was kneeling and attentive so the emperor would speak to him. If we were attentive and humble, we would kneel before our Father, the Creator of the entire universe, and say, "What is my Master's bidding?"

Remember, why does God want to speak to you? Because He likes you. He's absolutely crazy about you. Don't just go through life on the fast track to success. If you're not listening to God, you're on a fast track to failure.

As humans we often think we know what we need and know what we want. "I want this speaker system. I want this car with a radio, with a tape player, with a CD player. I want, I want, I want, I want." In the book of John, Pilate gave the Pharisees a choice. They thought they knew what they wanted. Pilate said to the Pharisees, "You can choose between Jesus or this thief. We'll give you the choice to let either the thief or Jesus go."

And what did the Pharisees choose? They chose the thief. They said, "Crucify Jesus. We want Barabbas released." Just like the Pharisees, we think we know what we want, but is it the

truth? Ultimately, if what you desire isn't first and foremost Jesus, then you're going to miss out on the best God has to offer.

The Pharisees said, "We want the thief." And they crucified the Son of God. If they had known, if they would have had the choice again, do you think they would have made the same decision?

What we really need is God, not our wants. If you will cultivate your communication with God, you will know what you truly need and what your heart really wants. If you cultivate your relationship with God, you won't be just a needy person looking for something to fill the void. Your needs will be met through your relationship with God.

> *When you put God first, everything else falls in line. If we will listen, pay attention, be grateful, and treasure His words, we'll get the rest of the things we desire, but more importantly, we'll get what our heart truly craves, our Creator.*

> ■ MATTHEW 6:33 MESSAGE

PRAYER ASKING GOD TO HELP YOU HEAR HIS VOICE AND DO THE THINGS THAT PLEASE HIM

Father God, my heart's desire is to hear You and please You with the things I do and say. I thank You for sending the Holy Spirit to remind me of the things I can do to make myself more open to Your voice. I choose to put You first and to listen, be obedient, pay attention, and give You thanks for all You are and do. I pray that I will come to know *You more as I listen and You speak to my heart. In Jesus' name, amen.* (John 14:26.)

HOW TO ENCOURAGE GOD TO SPEAK TO YOU

- Listen
- Be attentive
- Be obedient
- Be grateful
- Treasure God's words

Revival

Revival of the Bible

QUESTIONS FOR DISCUSSION AND REFLECTION

1. What are some of the things you can do to make yourself more aware of God's voice?

2. What are some of the ways you tune out and cause yourself to miss God's voice?

3. Has God spoken something to your heart and you haven't yet obeyed Him? What did He say?

4. What obstacles in your life might be keeping you from obeying God?

5. What can you do to show God that you treasure His words?

Section Two:

The Bible Applies to Everyday Life

Chapter Five

Where Was God When . . .?

God never leaves us. Even in our darkest moments, when we feel He is far away, He is right there with us. He gives us many signs, but when we begin to feel abandoned, we become deaf to His voice and blind to the signs of His presence around us. We begin to take on an abandoned mentality.

God wants us to live a life of abundance, not abandonment. After the death of Jesus, many of His followers felt abandoned, but Jesus appeared to them and reminded them of what He had promised. God promises to do the same for us.

"For what great nation is there that has God so near to it, as the Lord our God is to us, for whatever reason we may call upon Him?"

■ DEUTERONOMY 4:7

Have you ever felt as if you were walking along, minding your own business, and everything was going great? Then all of a sudden—*whoosh!*—you felt like the rug was pulled out from under you. You think, *What is happening to me?* I want to help you learn to move beyond the question, *Where was God when…?*

A BEIRUT BATHROOM

I remember one time when I was growing up, we went to Beirut, Lebanon. It was the first time I had been overseas. My parents had prepped me very carefully. One thing they made very, very clear was that I was never to leave the group for any reason. They threatened me within an inch of my life with these words: "You cannot leave the group." I was only five years old at the time, so my dad carried me everywhere on his shoulders. I loved it! It was great.

One evening we were having dinner in a hotel and I had to go to the bathroom. So I told my parents where I was going and then went down the hall to the restroom. The restrooms there aren't quite what we're accustomed to, of course, but I walked in and closed the door. It was one of those self-contained bathrooms where you couldn't slip under the door or anything. It was completely enclosed. I locked the door, went to the restroom, and when I was ready to leave, I tried to open the door. It wouldn't open. I was locked in.

I panicked. I was only five years old, and I felt so small at that moment. I was frightened, scared out of my mind. And of course the longer I was in there, the worse it got. I beat on the door and cried, "Help! Let me out! Help!" I banged on the door as hard as I could. Finally, I noticed a little window behind the toilet, so I thought I'd just climb up there and crawl out of the window. It was on the second floor, but I thought maybe there would be some way I could get down.

When I looked out the window, I saw a man standing next to a tank. He was holding his rifle and looking up at me. I scrambled back to the door and banged harder and harder and yelled at the top of my lungs, "HELP!"

Finally, I guess my brother heard me. He said, "It sounds like some kid is being beaten. Mom? Dad? Is that Sarah?" And so, at last, they came and rescued me. My heart was just pounding. I thought it would beat right out of my chest. I felt so abandoned. What happened? Where were my parents when I needed them?

We sometimes feel the same way as adults. Life begins to close in on us; we feel the rug being pulled out from under us, and we wonder, *God! Where are You?* Oftentimes, if we don't resolve those things, they begin to drive our behavior.

THE ABANDONMENT MENTALITY

I was talking with a friend of mine who works with foster children in Australia, and I asked her, "What are the most common characteristics of abandonment? How do people who are abandoned behave?"

She said, "People who feel abandoned are often angry. They're angry that they've been left alone. They may be physically angry or they may be passively angry. They push all their anger inside. They step back from people and detach themselves from life. Since they feel abandoned, they never connect with others in order to protect themselves from ever feeling abandoned again. They isolate themselves as a way of self-preservation. They disengage from life.

"They don't trust people. They feel like everyone has let them down, and they don't want to give anyone the chance to do it again. Sometimes these individuals become very secretive. They've been hurt, so they protect themselves by locking themselves away from the world. Additionally, they're afraid of commitment, because that makes them vulnerable. They think, *Well, last time I committed—the last time I loved—the rug was pulled out from under me.* Therefore, they're afraid to commit."

CHARACTERISTICS OF ABANDONMENT

- ANGER

- DETACHMENT

- ISOLATION

- DISTRUST

- SECRETIVENESS

- FEAR OF COMMITMENT

- CODEPENDENCY, OVER-PLEASING, OVERWORKING

This feeling of abandonment drives other people to become codependent. They try to over-please people. They work, work, work to make sure they do everything just right. The least bit of displeasure expressed toward them is very traumatic. They're afraid that if they do something wrong, everyone will leave them again.

These behaviors reflect an abandonment mentality. And the truth is, God does not want you to live the abandoned life, but rather the abundant life.

ABANDONMENT IN THE BIBLE

There are many examples in the Bible of people who felt abandoned by God. The disciples, for example, had been with Jesus day in and day out. They saw phenomenal miracles: Lazarus raised from the dead, multitudes healed, water turned to wine, and bread and fish multiplied. Jesus had warned them that He would be going away, but He promised He would come back to them. But when Jesus died, they wondered, *Why did He have to go?*

We can look at their behavior after Jesus' death and recognize some of the characteristics of abandonment. There are some specific instances where we can see this mentality very clearly. They wondered what had happened to Jesus' promises. They were angry and confused. *Why did He leave us like that?*

The first one is in Luke 24:13-35. Two of Jesus' disciples were walking along the road to Emmaus, discussing all the things that had just taken place in Jerusalem. As they were talking, a stranger joined them and asked them what they were talking about. They said, "Are you the only one in Jerusalem who hasn't heard what's happened during the last few days?" (Luke 24:18 MESSAGE).

> They began to explain the things that had taken place and Jesus showed them Scriptures from the Law and the Prophets why those things had to happen. When they came to the edge of the village, Jesus acted as if He was going to keep going, but they asked Him to eat with them.
>
> And here is what happened: He sat down at the table with them. Taking the bread, he blessed and broke and gave it to them. At that moment, open-eyed, wide-eyed, they recognized him. And then he disappeared. Back and forth they talked. "Didn't we feel on fire as he conversed with us on the road, as he opened up the Scriptures for us?"
>
> ■ LUKE 24:30-35 MESSAGE

They thought they were talking to a stranger. They were detached; they thought Jesus had abandoned them, but He was walking right there with them, conversing with them.

How many times does that happen to us? We think God has abandoned us but He's been right there with us all the time, and we can't see it until later? It wasn't until they sat down to eat and Jesus broke the bread. Then their eyes were opened and they could see who He really was. Jesus' breaking bread was something they had seen before, and it clicked with them. Suddenly they recognized Him.

It's when Jesus does things repetitively, things He's done in the past, that we can see Him again. Those things help us recognize He never left us; He was there all the time.

A simple example of this repetition that reminds us He's there happened to me a couple of years ago. A new mall had been built in Denver, and the first time I walked into it, I felt a very keen sense of the presence of God. Now, I'm not a shopper. It wasn't a sense of awe like, *Wow! A new mall!* I'm the type who goes into the mall, I get what I need, and I leave. So to sense God's presence in that place felt very bizarre to me, but I'll take God's presence anywhere I can get it. The next time I went into this mall the same thing happened, and the next time as well. God will repeat Himself to us over and over to remind us He's always there.

Another example of this is when God speaks something to me in my heart, and then later when I'm speaking to a friend, she will say the same thing to me. That repetition is one of the ways God shows us that He's ever present.

THE DISCIPLES GO FISH

I think this is really tragic, but I love this story because it reflects humanity. The disciples felt very abandoned and discouraged. *God, where did You go?* Jesus, You left us. Oftentimes when people feel detached, they begin to neglect church. They think God has left them, so they're going to leave Him.

The disciples had chosen to live the abandoned life. *Well, Jesus left us, so I'm checking out. I'm going to go back to fishing.*

Seven of the eleven disciples did exactly that. Jesus never called them to fish for fish; He called them to fish for men. But they disengaged, they detached, they disconnected from the call because they felt abandoned.

They were out fishing in the boat and saw someone on shore. They had no idea it was Jesus. He yelled out to them, "If you throw your net to the other side, you'll catch some fish." When they did, they caught a massive haul of fish. And the Bible specifically says, "Their nets did not break." (Luke 5:6.)

They finally realized that it was Jesus standing there on the shore. When did they recognize Him? When He provided. Peter jumped into the water and swam to shore because He wanted to be with Jesus.

So the second way God shows us that He's always with us is through provision. How many times do we take for granted even the smallest things God provides? Even simple things can speak of God's presence with us. Things like when my husband remembers to stock the refrigerator with my favorite fruit smoothies. I'm thankful to Reece, but I know that God is the real provider.

How often do we open the refrigerator and get our food or get in our car and put fuel in the tank and forget where it all comes from? We drive to work and receive our paycheck, and we tend to think we did it all ourselves, but we can't. God is our provider.

I remember one time a friend and I made a huge fruit salad for the two of us—a huge bowl heaped over with all of my favorite fruit. I thought it came through my work and effort, but it was God's provision. It was God's way of saying, *I love you Sarah, I've never left you.*

The third way God shows us He never leaves us is by proving to us that He's ever present. God is always progressive; He saves the best for last. I love the following story because God is so gracious. He shows us our humanity and His redemption.

Mary has gone to the tomb to anoint Jesus' body. He has just died and she's feeling abandoned. When she arrives at the tomb, she sees that the stone has been rolled away. Then she does something very strange. She leaves. She doesn't look inside to see if He's there. She leaves to go tell the disciples that the stone has been rolled away.

As soon as John and Peter hear about it, they take off for the tomb. John gets there first. He sees that the stone is rolled away, but he doesn't stop there. He looks inside. Then when Peter arrives, he takes it a step further. He goes all the way inside the tomb to examine the evidence.

Mary sees the stone rolled away, John bends over to look in and sees that no one is there, but Peter walks inside the tomb and examines the scene. He sees the face cloth folded but no body. Jesus was gone.

Mary, John, and Peter's reactions demonstrate the steps we follow when we have an abandonment mentality. Initially, we're curious. We think, *What happened? Where did God go?* Then we become more observant. Like John, we look in and say, "Yep. He's gone."

But then we get closer to that feeling of abandonment. We believe it a little bit more. It is a progression, a small but steady decline. We don't believe it all at once, but little by little we do. It's subtle.

Mary observed from a distance. John was a little more curious. First of all you think, *Oh well, He's not here.* Then you start to chew that and ponder it a little bit more.

I remember in my first semester of my junior year of college I felt as if God had left me, but I just kept trudging along. I thought, *Okay, I'm plugging my way through this.* By second semester I began to explore some of that abandonment feeling. I was more curious about it. Then finally I was like Peter, and I sought to prove that God had left me. Peter was intent on proving that the tomb was empty, that Jesus was no longer there. I had chosen to do the same thing. I believed the lie of abandonment rather than choosing the abundant life. That's exactly what happened with Mary, John, and Peter.

Now watch this. John and Peter proved that Jesus had left them. So they've decided it's settled. They leave and go back to the other disciples, but Mary stays behind, weeping.

> *Jesus said to her, "Woman, why are you weeping? Whom are you seeking?" She, supposing Him to be the gardener, said to Him, "Sir, if You have carried Him away, tell me where You have laid Him, and I will take Him away." Jesus said to her, "Mary!" She turned and said to Him, "Rabboni!" (which is to say, Teacher).*

> ■ JOHN 20:15,16

She didn't recognize Him until He said, "Mary." When He calls your name, you recognize the fact that He never left you. I believe that God is consistently and continually calling us, drawing us, beckoning us, calling our names. Isaiah tells us:

Listen to me, all of you in far-off lands! The Lord called me before my birth; from within the womb he called me by name.

■ ISAIAH 49:1 NLT

He made mention of your name in your mother's womb. He is continually calling your name. Mary recognized Him when He called her name. Mary said, "It's You." But He was there all the time, talking to her; she just didn't recognize Him.

Knowing someone's name reflects relationship. When you hear Him calling your name, it reflects abundance, not abandonment.

Sometimes people come up to me and say, "Oh, you're Marilyn Hickey's daughter."

I say, "Yes, and your name is?"

"Harry."

"Oh, Harry, it's nice to meet you. I'm Sarah."

Then we have a relationship. A relationship begins when you know someone's name and they know yours. That relationship reflects abundance, not abandonment.

In John 10:3 Jesus said:

"To him the doorkeeper opens, and the sheep hear his voice; and he calls his own sheep by name."

You are His sheep, and He calls you by name. The Lord said to Moses in Exodus 33:17:

"I will also do this thing that you have spoken; for you have found grace in my sight, and I know you by name."

He knows your name. In Isaiah 40:26 it says:

87

"Lift up your eyes on high, see who has created these things, who brings out their host by number; He calls them all by name."

God has never left us. He reveals Himself to us by repetitively doing things He's done in the past. He repeats them again and again because He wants us to recognize that He has never left us. When we're wondering, *Where was God when...*, He's always there.

In each of these three instances, Jesus was right there with His disciples and they didn't know it. They couldn't see Him. That's what happens to us. We ask God why He left us, and He says, *I was there all along, you just couldn't see Me.* The truth is, He never leaves us.

WAYS GOD SHOWS YOU HE IS WITH YOU

- HE REPEATS THINGS HE HAS DONE FOR YOU IN THE PAST.

- HE PROVIDES FOR YOUR EVERY NEED.

- HE DELIGHTS IN PROVING TO YOU THAT HE'S EVER PRESENT.

- HE KNOWS YOUR NAME AND CALLS YOU BY NAME.

God is there even when we don't recognize Him. There are many things we can look to that remind us God is always with us. We may not always sense His presence, but there are things around us that consistently tell us God is there.

God also shows us that He is with us by His provision; He gives things to us all the time. Also, He shows us He's with us by continually calling our name. He knows six billion names, and each of them is equally important to Him. Each of our names is inscribed on His hands. (Isa. 49:16.) How big His hands must be to fit all those names!

ABANDONED IN GERMANY

When I was a junior at Oral Roberts University, I left the country and went to study in Germany for the summer. I had just come through a pretty tough year and was struggling in my heart. I had been feeling very lonely, and I wasn't hearing from God. I felt depressed, discouraged, and despondent.

I was staying in a beautiful little town in southwestern Germany, but it was very isolated. I was living with a family just on the outskirts of the town. The whole situation magnified my discouragement tremendously. The longer I was there, the more discouraged I became. The lonelier I felt, the more dissatisfied I became. It was really a difficult time, and I didn't feel that God was talking to me.

I tried to talk to God. I tried to hear from Him. I tried to stay in the Word, but everything was dry and dead. The Word was no longer vibrant and alive to me. I began to have bad dreams. I was struggling in every area of my life.

Finally, toward the end of my time in Germany, I said, "God, I feel like You have left me. You have abandoned me. Where are You?" I didn't feel as if I got any kind of answer, and that made me very angry, so I rejected God. I completely turned away from Him and said that I didn't believe in Christianity anymore. I decided that maybe I was a Christian just because I was born in America. If I were in India, I would probably be Hindu, or if I had been born in China, I would be a Buddhist.

When I came back to the U.S., I spoke with my Mom and told her where I was spiritually. I was very honest with her about my feelings. I told her that I was no longer a Christian. I told her that I wanted to know truth but I no longer believed in Christianity. My mom was very affirming and gentle.

She said, "Regardless of what you believe, we love you. We loved you when you were a baby and you didn't believe in anything. That has never changed and never will." But she also said, "I know when you come through this, you will be a stronger Christian at the end than you ever were before."

I went back to ORU and began to search for the truth. I asked over and over, "God, where are You? Who are You? Do You exist? Do You care about me? What is life? What is the relationship between life and God? Where am I? What is my purpose? Who am I on this planet?" I began to really search.

To make a long story short, I eventually came back to Christ that school year. I chose to renew my life to Him, but the gnawing sense in the back of my mind had not completely gone. I kept wondering what had happened in Germany. Why did I have to go through that? I came to the point where I just didn't allow myself to think about it anymore. I knew that one day God would help me resolve those issues.

Several years later I was in Australia. I was spending some time alone in prayer and having great fellowship with God. I felt God had given me a sermon on abandonment, and as I was working on it, I felt it was time to ask again. "God, where were You when I was in Germany? I felt so abandoned. What happened?"

As I worked through the sermon, God started showing me how He had been with me all the time. He took me back to a night in Germany when I was lying in my bed, discouraged and upset. I was so mad at Him, but I was still trying to find Him. God said, *You turned your back on Me, but I was right there sitting in the room with you.* He said, *I never left you. My Word says I will never leave you or forsake you, and I did not leave you, Sarah. You thought I left you. You turned away from Me, but I never left you.* (Heb. 13:5.)

He showed me the room. He was sitting right there, and He was crying even more than I was because I had believed a lie. Seeing that picture of God weeping over me because I had believed that He abandoned me brought the restoration and reconciliation I needed. He had been with me all the time. And He is with you. No matter what you're going through or how abandoned you feel, He's right there. Don't turn away.

Sometimes we feel that when the rug has been pulled out from under us, there's nothing left. But usually under a rug you find carpet or tile; under the carpet or tile there's a cement foundation;

and under that foundation is the ground. Finally, under that dirt you eventually come to rock. At that point, you're standing directly on the rock, Jesus Christ.

> *Come, let's shout praises to God, raise the roof for the Rock who saved us!*

> ■ PSALM 95:1 MESSAGE

The Rock is never pulled out from under you. He never leaves you. Never.

How many times do we want to be convinced rather than live by conviction? We say, "Prove it," instead of "I believe it." The abundant life comes through believing in God's promises, rather than living an abandoned life. He has never left us. He is calling us by name.

PRAYER TO RECOGNIZE THE SIGNS THAT GOD IS WITH ME EVERYWHERE I GO

Father God, I thank You that You've promised to be with me always, everywhere I go. Open my eyes. Help me to see the signs that You're there, especially when I feel so far away from You. You are my hiding place, my safe refuge. I thank You that You never leave me or forsake me. I cling to Your promise. In Jesus' name, amen. (Matt.28:20; Ps. 32:7; 119:114; 62:7; 91:2; Heb. 13:5.)

QUESTIONS FOR DISCUSSION AND REFLECTION

1. Can you see any of the characteristics of abandonment in your own life? Which ones?

2. In this chapter there are some examples of people in the Bible who felt abandoned by God; there are many more examples in the Word. Can you think of some? If you can't think of any, read the stories of Job and David. Read the Psalms. What characteristics of abandonment do you see in their stories?

3. What are some of the ways God proves to you that He is always with you? Can you think of some examples in your own life?

4. What are the signs of an abandonment mentality? Are you walking out any of those steps right now?

5. God knows your name. Meditate on the Scriptures given in this chapter. When you feel the rug has been pulled out from under you, what are you left standing on?

Chapter Six

How Do I Find Success Through the Storms of Life?

We all face storms in life. If we choose to handle them God's way, they can make us stronger. However, if we choose to disobey God, the storm may just swallow us up. The stories of two men from the Bible, Jonah and Paul, demonstrate to us two very different ways of handling the storms in our lives. We can choose, like Jonah, to end up as fish food, or with God's help, using five gauges to measure our success in the storm, we can encourage those around us and end up like Paul. He reached his final destination victoriously!

STORMY WEATHER

I was talking with a friend of mine recently, and he told me about all the major storms he was facing in his life. He and his family were planning to go on vacation and had put down a $500 deposit on a hotel room. However, due to some problems with their flight, they were unable to make their reservation. The hotel refused to refund their money, so they lost the $500.

Shortly after that, his wife got sick. Then she lost her contacts. Next, they found out they had to move out of their home. He then found out his mother had to have emergency surgery, and he was beginning to feel sick himself.

I bet we could all tell similar stories. As in nature, life goes in cycles. There are different seasons, and one season is usually more prone to storms than another. Therefore, the storms are an inevitable part of life, but there are two possible outcomes to every storm. You will either survive it victoriously, or you will become fish food.

We battle many different kinds of storms in life. Oftentimes things are going along fine, and then—*bam!*—it hits you. Not just a little problem here and there, but a deluge, a flood. When it rains, it pours. It all seems to come against you at once.

Maybe it's marriage problems. Maybe your mate recently told you that he or she wants a divorce. Or maybe you recently found out that your spouse has been unfaithful. That's a marital storm.

Maybe you found out that you have a serious medical condition. Maybe one of your parents has been diagnosed with a terminal disease. Maybe you recently received a phone call from your teenager's school, saying, "Sorry, would you please come collect your son or your daughter because he or she has tried to commit suicide." That's a physical and emotional storm.

You may say, "Well, I just got my car paid off, but now I found out I have a health insurance bill that I didn't know was due.

And my car fell apart. I had to put in a fuel pump, and then my heater broke down." That's a financial storm.

Many of us even deal with the storm of insecurity. We don't like to admit it, but there are times when we feel extremely insecure. Things that come against us intimidate us, and we want to shrink back and hide. We all have these difficult times in our lives, but God has planned for us to be successful through every storm we face.

You may try to put on a brave face and pretend everything is okay when your life is a hurricane. But God wants you to know that you can come out on the other side of your storm with success and victory. God in you is bigger than any storm. There is no storm so large that God and you cannot handle it. By yourself, you have the choice of becoming fish food or just barely surviving. But God in you will cause you to do more than just barely survive; you will have success and victory through the storm.

TWO MEN, TWO STORMS, TWO OUTCOMES

There are two great stories in the Bible about handling storms. One story shows how not to handle a storm, the other shows not only how to come out on the other side victoriously, but also how to be triumphant in the midst of the storm. Jonah and Paul were in similar circumstances. Both men were traveling by boat, and they both found themselves in the midst of a terrible storm at sea.

JONAH'S STORM

"Arise, go to Nineveh, that great city, and cry out against it; for their wickedness has come up before Me."

■ JONAH 1:2

God called Jonah and told him to go to Nineveh to preach the gospel, so the people there would repent. But, instead, Jonah chose to get on a boat going in the opposite direction.

But Jonah arose to flee to Tarshish from the presence of the Lord. He went down to Joppa, and found a ship going to Tarshish; so he paid the fare, and went down into it, to go with them to Tarshish from the presence of the Lord.

■ JONAH 1:3

After they had been at sea for a while, a great storm came up, but Jonah was in the bottom of the boat sleeping.

The Lord sent a great wind on the sea, and there was a mighty tempest on the sea, so that the ship was about to be broken up. Then the mariners were afraid; and every man cried out to his god, and threw the cargo that was in the ship into the sea, to lighten the load. But Jonah had gone down into the lowest parts of the ship, had lain down, and was fast asleep.

■ JONAH 1:4,5

The men on board found Jonah sleeping and asked him to pray. Somehow these men knew that Jonah was a man of God, but he wasn't acting like it. Jonah didn't seem to care that they were most likely going to drown. Finally, the men asked Jonah to please do something. Jonah's reaction was to continue to run from God, so he told the men to throw him overboard.

"Pick me up and throw me into the sea; then the sea will become calm for you. For I know that this great tempest is because of me."

■ JONAH 1:12

At first the men did not want to throw Jonah overboard. Perhaps they feared punishment from Jonah's God. The storm would not relent, however, and they were facing sure death anyway, so they finally threw Jonah over the side of the boat. God had a fish there waiting to swallow Jonah, and he spent three days and nights in the belly of the fish. Finally, Jonah repented and the fish spit him out on the shore of Nineveh. Jonah obeyed God and Nineveh repented.

PAUL'S STORM

We find Paul's story in Acts 27. He had been ambushed and arrested by the Jews for preaching the gospel, but as a Roman citizen, Paul appealed to Caesar. So he was now on his way to Rome to present his case to him. When they were far out to sea, a tempest blew up that lasted for several days.

Now when neither sun nor stars appeared for many days, and no small tempest beat on us, all hope that we would be saved was finally given up. But after long abstinence from food, then Paul stood in the midst of them and said, "Men, you should have listened to me, and not have sailed from Crete and incurred this disaster and loss. And now I urge you to take heart, for there will be no loss of life among you, but only of the ship. For there stood by me this night an angel of the God to whom I belong and whom I serve, saying, 'Do not be afraid, Paul; you must be brought before Caesar; and indeed God has granted you all those who sail with you.' Therefore take heart, men, for I believe God that it will be just as it was told me."

■ Acts 27:20-25

Paul is going through a horrific storm. This storm is so bad that on the second day the sailors had to stretch ropes underneath the boat to keep it from breaking apart. Then they began to throw out their supplies. First they threw their tools overboard, then their cargo, and eventually their food. They did everything they could think of just to survive. They were facing a terrifying storm, but Paul knew that God was bigger than any storm.

FIVE GAUGES TO MEASURE YOUR SUCCESS IN A STORM

Now, using Jonah and Paul's stories as examples, I want to show you five gauges you can use to measure your success in any storm. Gauges in a boat, car, or machine indicate how things are operating. They tell you if your car is overheating, if you're running out of fuel, or if you're going in the right direction. They're indicators of the machine's success in carrying out its function.

God has promised success in the midst of your storms, and you can use these five gauges to be sure you know which way you're going and if you're functioning properly. They will tell you if you're going to end up as fish food or if you're going to be victorious. God wants you to be successful in your storm, so He's given you these indicators to keep you on course.

Gauge 1: What caused the storm?

In Jonah's case, the storm was caused by nothing but his own disobedience. The reason Paul was in a storm is simply because it was the season for storms. When a storm comes your way, you have to ask yourself: *Have I been disobedient? Is there something God has asked me to do that I haven't done? Is there something I'm doing that God has told me not to do?* It's easy to think it's just an attack from the devil and not accept responsibility, but sometimes we have opened the door by our disobedience.

Therefore, the first thing to do when you're experiencing a storm is to examine yourself. If you have been disobedient, repent and obey God. If you're honest with yourself, you know in your heart God told you that you should or shouldn't do something. So sometimes our storm is caused by our own willfulness.

There are other times in our lives when storms come simply because it's storm season. As I mentioned before, just like there are seasons in nature, our lives cycle through seasons. My friend mentioned at the beginning of the chapter was in a storm season. Those kinds of storms can make us stronger in our faith if we let God take us through them. Just check your gauge to make sure you're not disobeying God.

Gauge 2: What is your attitude in the storm?

Jonah's attitude was to isolate himself. He went down into the bottom of the ship and fell asleep, hoping it would all just go away. He didn't want to deal with God or anyone else, so he chose to isolate himself. When we're facing a major storm in our lives, we tend to want to do the same. We stop going to church. We stop going to Bible study. We want to go home where we feel somewhat safe and secure and we can escape. The storm is whirling around us and we just want to get away from it. That's what Jonah chose to do.

In contrast, Paul was right there in the thick of it with the other men on board the ship. He stood up in the middle of the boat and encouraged everyone. The storm was raging all around him, and he told the men not to worry, that everything would be okay.

After you've checked the first gauge, *Am I being obedient?* you can check the second gauge, *What is my attitude? Am I isolating myself, or am I boldly standing up and encouraging myself and those around me?* When we isolate ourselves, we're saying that the storm is bigger than God on the inside of us is. What a lie! Do not buy into that lie.

People are watching you to learn how to behave in a storm. They may know all the things you're going through and decide to watch you to see how you handle it. Your neighbors, your coworkers, your parents, your children—they're all watching to see how you'll behave. If you smile in the midst of the storm and stand up, courageously encouraging others, they'll see you living the things you talk about. God in you is bigger than any storm.

Gauge 3: How am I treating the people around me?

Jonah treated the people around him with indifference. He didn't really care what happened to them. He just wanted to get away from God. That kind of attitude will sink you in a hurry.

Paul, on the other hand, was extremely concerned about the men with him in the boat. He was very interactive. He told them that God was with them and that they would make it through safely. Paul listened to what the angel told him and shared it with everyone else. He told them to eat something and to rest because everything would be okay.

When we're in a storm, we tend to get so self-focused that we miss God's heart for people. He is very concerned about the people in your life. He's so concerned about them, He sent *you* to them. Not me; not Marilyn Hickey, not Benny Hinn, not Reece Bowling, not Wallace Hickey—He sent you. He cared enough about the people in your life to send *you* to them. So when you're facing a storm, don't let yourself become indifferent about the people God has placed in your life. Remember His heart for those people. They're watching you. You're a living example for them so they can learn how, and be encouraged, to handle the storms in their own lives.

Gauge 4: What effect does your presence have on the people around you?

When Jonah was in the boat, his presence was very dangerous to those around him. As long as he was on board, everyone else was at risk. Paul's presence on the boat was a lifesaver. Paul was a preserver. There were 275 people in the boat, plus himself, and he was a life preserver to all of those people. Paul stood up and said, "Because I'm here, everyone else will be saved. Because God in me is bigger than any storm, you'll be safe."

Check your gauge. In your storm, are you dangerous? Are people going to drown? Will they die without hearing about Jesus?

Are they going to perish without any hope in their life? Or are you a life preserver? When you consistently check your gauges in the storm, you act as a life preserver. You give those around you hope and encouragement. I can picture Paul wearing a life preserver around his neck and all those men hanging on to him. He is saving their lives from the storm.

I want to encourage you: God in you is bigger than any doctor's report. God in you is bigger than any problems with your children. God in you is bigger than your mate's telling you he or she wants a divorce. God in you is bigger than your employer telling you you're fired. *God in you is bigger than any storm!*

I remember when I first met my husband, his parents had just died. He was going through a terrible storm. His family was trying to settle the estate, and there was discord within his family. But God in Reece was bigger than that storm, and he emerged victorious, able to be an example and encouragement to his family.

Think about the storms in your life right now. What storm or storms are you facing? Identify the storm, then hold it up to God and watch it shrink.

There's a really fun and easy method for measuring the height of a tree without climbing it. Just cut a stick the same length as your arm. Then stand in front of the tree, holding the stick parallel to the tree at arm's length in your line of vision. Then walk backward until the stick looks like it is the same size as the tree. Then simply measure the distance from the base of the tree to the spot where the stick looked the same size as the tree and you'll find the tree's height.

In order to use this method, you have to keep your focus on the stick. If you shift your focus to the tree, your perspective changes and the tree looks big again, and the stick, small. You could never measure how big God is, so just keep your focus on Him and you'll see the reality: He is much bigger than your storm!

Gauge 5: Where are you going after the storm?

I call this one the ATS gauge (After The Storm).

So you've checked gauges one through four: obedience, attitude, how you treat people, and the effect of your presence. Now there's just one more gauge to check.

Jonah was despondent; he had no particular destination in mind. He just wanted to get as far away from God as he could, although he knew that was impossible. He basically said, "I'd rather kill myself than turn around. Throw me into the ocean."

Well, compare that with Paul. What did Paul's ATS gauge indicate? He was full of faith. Paul had plans. He was on his way to see Caesar. Caesar was one of the most powerful men on earth at the time, and Paul's plan was to use this as an opportunity to witness to him about Jesus Christ. He was going to give Caesar the gospel.

When we're in the midst of the storm, the tendency is to just hold on with everything we've got. We have no thought of where we're headed; we just want to get through the storm in one piece. But God wants you to look beyond the storm. Where are you going? Where does God want you to go? He will get you there, no matter how big the storm looks.

Five Ways To Gauge Your Success in a Storm

Gauge 1: What caused the storm?

Gauge 2: What is your attitude in the storm?

Gauge 3: How am I treating the people around me?

Gauge 4: What effect does your presence have on the people around you?

Gauge 5: Where are you going after the storm?

SUCCESS TACTICS TO TAKE YOU THROUGH THE STORM

Success Tactic 1: "Tack" between the Word of God and prayer.

Tacking is a sailing term. When I was a teenager, I was a crew member on a little boat. We had races at the local reservoir. I learned that when you steer a sailboat, you don't go in a straight line. You tack. You go a little ways in one direction, and when you've made some progress, you shift the sails and the rudder around and go a little to the left or right. Eventually, after tacking this way and that, you arrive at your destination. You're using the wind to take you back and forth, but you end up in the right spot.

In the storm, instead of a sail and a rudder, you have the Word of God and prayer. If you tack back and forth between spending time in the Word and spending time in prayer, you'll maintain the proper course. If you consistently have both prayer and the Word in your life, you will get through the storm and reach your destination. Prayer and the Word work together and are mutually reinforcing. Therefore, you've got to have both prayer and the Word, or you'll tack too far in one direction or the other and you'll miss your dock.

Success Tactic 2: See through the storm by focusing on your destination.

God has promised you a future:

For I know the thoughts that I think toward you, says the Lord, thoughts of peace and not of evil, to give you a future and a hope.

■ JEREMIAH 29:11

What is your destination?

Look past the storm. Look past the curve in the trail and take note of where you're headed. Look past the block in front of you, and see your hand punched through to the other side. Push your way forward by looking past the obstacles. God has a good plan for your life. Look toward that plan. Don't get stuck in the storm and become fish food.

LOOK THROUGH THE CURVE

One day I was talking with a friend of mine. We were discussing some of the different techniques we've used to work through the storms we've faced. I remember one time I was up in the mountains taking a mountain-biking clinic, and I was on a really cool single trail. It was the kind of trail where you race along bouncing over boulders and dodging tree limbs. I looked up at the people ahead of me and saw them approaching a hairpin curve. Then a lump began to form in my throat as I watched one after another miss the curve and fly off the trail.

My instructor came up behind me and pointed out the people flipping over their handlebars. He said, "You think you're going to be next, right?" I nodded vigorously. But as we approached the curve, he kept saying, "Look through the curve. Look through the curve." The people who had flipped over their handlebars were focusing so intently on the curve that they couldn't turn. My instructor said, "Look past the curve. Look at where you're going to go." He said, "Where you look is where you're going to wind up."

I did what he said, but it was really scary. It was hard not to look at the curve. I wanted to watch where I was going at that moment.

He said, "No, look at where you're going to go." And where I looked is exactly where I went. I made the curve. Hallelujah! Where you look is where you're going to end up.

I have a friend who is a black belt in Tae Kwon Do. We were talking about this principle one day, and I told her about my mountain-biking experience.

She said, "You know, that's interesting. It's the same principle I use to break blocks." She said she had seen people try to break a block and hit it so hard that their knuckles smashed back into their wrists. But she had learned the secret of avoiding such an injury. She said that you look past the block. You see the block in front of you, but you look beyond it, because that is where you want your punch to go. That's where you want your hand to end up.

Success Tactic 3: Save people along the way.

God isn't keeping you through the storm just so you can barely squeak through it. He is bringing you through the storm so you can live in victory and bring others along with you. Paul saved 275 people on his boat, and beyond that, when they reached Malta, there was a huge revival. Paul had the opportunity to pray for the ruler of the island, and revival broke out. Eventually, Paul reached his destination, stood before Caesar, and witnessed to the most powerful man in the world. But he didn't hold back his witness until he reached Caesar; he saved those he met along the way.

If God is for you, who can be against you? (Rom. 8:31.) No weapon formed against you can prosper. (Isa. 54:17.) You can do all things through Christ who strengthens you. (Phil. 4:13.) God supplies all of your needs according to His riches in glory. (Phil. 4:19.) You are the head and not the tail. (Deut. 28:13.) God has made all things that you put your hands to prosper. (Deut. 30:9.)

Live abundantly, live fully, live lavishly, and live richly in God's provision in your heart and life.

SUCCESS TACTICS FOR MAKING IT THROUGH THE STORM

TACTIC 1: "TACK" BETWEEN THE WORD OF GOD AND PRAYER.

TACTIC 2: SEE THROUGH THE STORM BY FOCUSING ON YOUR DESTINATION.

TACTIC 3: SAVE PEOPLE ALONG THE WAY. IT WILL HELP YOU SHIFT YOUR FOCUS FROM THE STORM TO THE DESTINATION.

PRAYER FOR GOD TO HELP ME SEE MY DESTINATION THROUGH THE STORM

Heavenly Father, I thank You that You do have a good plan for my life. Thank You for giving me hope for the future. I pray that You would show me my destination and enable me to focus on it in the midst of any storm that comes my way. Help me to behave as Paul did in the midst of the storm and encourage others, while keeping my eyes on the destination You have planned for me. Thank You for carrying me safely through every storm. In Jesus' name, amen. (Jer. 29:11.)

SCRIPTURES TO STAND ON IN THE MIDST OF THE STORM

So, what do you think? With God on our side like this, how can we lose?

■ ROMANS 8:31 MESSAGE

In that coming day, no weapon turned against you will succeed. And everyone who tells lies in court will be brought to justice. These benefits are enjoyed by the servants of the Lord; their vindication will come from me. I, the Lord, have spoken!

■ ISAIAH 54:17 NLT

I can do all things through Christ who strengthens me.

■ PHILIPPIANS 4:13

You can be sure that God will take care of everything you need, his generosity exceeding even yours in the glory that pours from Jesus.

■ PHILIPPIANS 4:19 MESSAGE

If you listen to these commands of the Lord your God and carefully obey them, the Lord will make you the head and not the tail, and you will always have the upper hand.

■ DEUTERONOMY 28:13 NLT

The Lord your God will make you abound in all the work of your hand, in the fruit of your body, in the increase of your livestock, and in the produce of your land for good. For the lord will again rejoice over you for good as He rejoiced over your fathers.

■ DEUTERONOMY 30:9

QUESTIONS FOR DISCUSSION AND REFLECTION

1. What are some storms you've faced in your life?

2. When you faced the storms, did you handle it like Jonah or like Paul?

3. Have you ever gone in the opposite direction God asked you to go? How did He bring you back to a place of obedience?

4. What did you learn from that experience?

5. What are some of the ways you can gauge your success in a storm? If you're currently experiencing a storm in your life, where do you stand?

6. What destination did Paul have in mind as he faced his storm? What's your destination?

7. What attitude do you tend to have when you're facing a storm? What can you do to make sure you have an encouraging attitude?

8. Has anyone ever told you they learned something from watching your behavior when you were in the midst of a storm? What did they learn?

Chapter Seven

How Do I Slay the Giants That Get in My Way?

The familiar story of David and Goliath can give us many clues as to what it takes to defeat our giants. Just as David chose five smooth stones to place in his arsenal, God has given us five smooth stones of wisdom to use in slaying our giants. As a child of God, when we learn to listen to the giants' threats and ignore those who would try to distract us from the real giant, as David did, we can hit the giant square in the head with our smooth stones, knock it down, and cut its head off!

SCRUBBING

When I was growing up, there was a neighborhood tradition that on the last week of school, all of the sixth graders were initiated into the seventh grade. There was an elaborate ritual that was very cruel and frightening, and it scared me out of my skull. It was called "scrubbing."

All of the seventh, eighth, and ninth graders—everyone who was older than you—would hide in the bushes near the bus stop after school. After you got off the bus and started walking home, they would jump out of the bushes, pin you to the ground, and cover every single bit of exposed flesh with lipstick. And they would do all kinds of other mean things to you—pour nail polish on you, pour glue in your hair, ruin your clothes, and take your books. I remember seeing this happen to kids when I was in the third, fourth, and fifth grades. It was very traumatic.

I felt so small compared to the seventh and eighth graders. I was petrified; I didn't want the school year to end because it brought me that much closer to seventh grade. To make matters worse, the bullies caught wind that I was scared, so they tormented me. "Hickey, we're coming after you! We're going to scrub you the best of anybody!" I felt like such a little person against these huge seventh and eighth graders. Me, the little underdog, versus the big neighborhood bullies.

I was so scared about approaching seventh grade. Every year I got older and the "scrubbing" got closer. I thought about it constantly, *What am I going to do?* Thankfully, God was good to me. I changed schools at the end of my fifth grade year. The "scrubbing" wasn't the only reason I changed schools, but nonetheless, I thought I'd been spared. Well, the neighborhood kids didn't care. They had my number. They said, "We don't care what grade you're going into! You better expect it at the end of your fifth grade year, because we're going to get you." I was scared and shaking day after day.

I was terrified that last week of school, but my parents found out what was happening. They found out I was scared, and so every morning for that last week, Dad would assure me, "Honey, I will be at your bus stop this afternoon to walk you home."

Yeah Dad! It was great. He kept his promise. He was there every day, so nobody scrubbed me.

Why would they scrub me with my dad walking right there beside me? I didn't even glance toward the bushes, because I wasn't nervous. My dad was right there. Even though I was the underdog, I overcame the neighborhood bullies because my dad was right there with me.

God wants you to know that He is your heavenly Father. He is walking right there beside you, and there is no bully, no giant, that can overwhelm His ability and His provision in your life.

THE GIANTS

You probably know the classic underdog story, David and Goliath. David was a scrawny little boy, but he took his stones in his slingshot, hit Goliath in the head, and Goliath fell. Then David rushed over and chopped his head off. But you want to know how to defeat the giants in your life today. Yes, the story of David and Goliath is a great story, but what about *your* giants?

You may have received a report from the doctor that says you have terminal cancer, and that giant is screaming at you, leering at you, mocking you, saying, *Your mother died of cancer, your grandmother died of cancer, your whole family has died of cancer, and you're next.* Maybe it's another health problem, and that giant is scream-ing at you and intimidating you. You feel like the underdog.

Maybe your kids are making bad decisions. It's a giant. It seems as if no matter what happens, your kids are constantly mak-ing bad decisions. No matter what you do, it seems like they are bent on destroying themselves. The giant taunts you and laughs at you.

Maybe your mate is not saved. Maybe you're trying to witness to him or her, and the more loving and kind you are, the worse he or she gets. That's a giant. It seems as if every time you come home and there's a conflict over God, that giant is laughing at you, jeering, *Oh, he'll never get saved...she'll always be a backslider. This'll never change....* And the more you're around the giant, the bigger it seems to get.

Maybe your giant is problems at work. Maybe your boss doesn't like you. The giant says, *I'm going to do everything within my power to keep you from getting a promotion. I'm going to make your work life miserable.* That's a giant laughing at you, and every year the promotions come around and the giant seems to laugh harder and louder and get bigger and stronger.

God wants you to know that you are not the underdog. You do not have to be the victim any longer; you are the victor! You are going to learn the mechanics of giant killing, but the main key to defeating your giant is to determine who is listening. Are you listening with your natural ears, as a mere mortal, or are you listening as a child of the living God? The "you" who is listening determines who wins.

David had a giant in his life. The giants that you face every day, those giants that laugh at you, are no less intimidating than the giant David faced. Your giants tell you, *You're worthless, you're a fool, you'll never amount to anything, your husband will always be a unbeliever, you'll always live in debt....* All these giants scream at you.

David faced the same kind of intimidation. Goliath was no wimp. He was over nine feet tall. Nine feet! Can you picture it? The tallest player in the NBA isn't even eight feet tall. Goliath was not just tall; he was a big guy. He wore a bronze helmet and scale armor that weighed over 150 pounds. He was well-protected and well-armed. The spear he carried was almost as thick as a telephone pole, and the arrowhead on the end weighed almost 20 pounds.

Your giants are no less intimidating. They are big, well-protected, and well-armed. But David overcame the giant, and so can you!

Not only does Goliath look intimidating, but he also says intimidating words. For forty days, Goliath stood against the Israelites and said to them, "Hey, let's not fight in a conventional way. Let's just bring out one guy from your side and one guy from mine. I'll be the one guy. We'll fight each other and end this war." He intimidated them for forty days with his words.

This is a key. Goliath was the enemy and was dictating the terms of battle, but David was able to beat Goliath on Goliath's terms! You can beat the Goliaths in your life, even on their own terms. When your husband or your wife says to you, "I will never go to church with you," watch God get him or her to church with a friend or relative. God defeats your enemy even on his own terms.

When the doctor says to you, "You've got cancer and you're going to die; there's nothing medicine can do for you," no problem. God can work a miracle and heal your body. When your kids say to you, "I'll never serve Christ. I'll never go to your church," watch God work in their lives through their friends. God says, *Fine, you want to dictate the terms? I can still win, even on your terms.* God will win even on the enemy's terms.

THE ISRAELITES' RESPONSE TO GOLIATH

All the men of Israel, when they saw the man, fled from him and were dreadfully afraid.

■ I SAMUEL 17:24

Now I want you to see this. Remember, who is listening determines who wins. The Israelites heard Goliath taunting them continuously for forty days. They responded first with fear, then they decided they would try and solve things with a conventional battle. We often do the same thing. We try to fight the giants in our lives using conventional means. But God says you cannot overcome an unconventional enemy using conventional methods.

The next thing the Israelites did was run away. They basically said, "Have you *seen* that guy? Whoever defeats him will be the greatest hero in all of Israel!" All of the Israelites, and there were thousands of them there, heard as mere mortals.

Are you listening to your giant as a mere mortal, or are you listening as a child of God? Listening as a child of God is the key to overcoming the giants in your life. When David arrived, he could hear Goliath too, but he heard him in a different way.

KAZAKHSTAN GIANT

Not too long ago, I faced a giant in my own life. I was in Kazakhstan on a ministry trip with my mother. One night she got really, really sick, to the point that she couldn't preach. I told her, "I'll do whatever I can to help you. If you want me to preach, I'll do that. I'll even stand on my head. I'll do whatever I can to help."

And she said, "Well, if you can preach, that would be great." I couldn't believe it. I was so concerned for my mother. She is rarely sick, and yet she was so sick she asked me to preach! I wondered how good the medicine was in Kazakhstan.

She asked me to preach! I thought, *Oh man, I've got to preach in front of three or four thousand people. They're expecting mom, not me.* That was intimidating. Furthermore, I had less than an hour to prepare. Then, when we got to the church service, there were some unusual, off-the-wall things happening.

As I was sitting there waiting to minister with all these unusual things going on, my time to preach was getting shorter and shorter and I was becoming more and more intimidated. The giant began to scream at me, *Who do you think you are? You think you're going to get up there having prepared in less than an hour and pull something miraculous out of your hat? Who do you think you are?*

The service kept getting more bizarre, and I looked to my mom for comfort, but that just made things worse. She looked horrible. The giant leered, *What are you going to do?*

I had to make a choice. Was I going to listen as the mortal daughter of Marilyn Hickey and have mortal results? *Mom's sick, the service is getting bizarre, there are three thousand people here, I've had no time to prepare, I have to use a translator...* and on and on. It just got worse. I had to decide. Was I going to continue to think that way, or was I going to listen as the daughter of the living God?

If I chose to listen as a mere mortal, I was going to get mortal results. But I chose not to listen to the intimidation and said, "Yeah, I hear you. You just keep talking your trash. Keep going. I'm not intimidated because I'm listening as the daughter of the living God. You watch and see what God will do here tonight!"

God, as always, was faithful. A lady came up and gave a testimony. She had had an ultrasound of her diseased ovaries before prayer and another ultrasound of her healthy ovaries after God had done a miracle. Another man came up who could not see clearly in his left eye, and as a result, he had been unable to read since he was a small child. I covered up his good eye and held a Bible in front of him, and he read using only his left eye. God did awesome miracles. And the biggest miracle of all is that about three or four hundred people came forward to receive Christ.

The giants will always be there, telling you, *You're a wimp, you're worthless, I'm gonna scrub you.* The key is not in the giant's words, but in who is listening to the words.

How did David hear Goliath? David was indignant.

*David spoke to the men who stood by him, saying, "What shall
be done for the man who kills this Philistine and takes away the
reproach from Israel? For who is this uncircumcised Philistine,
that he should defy the armies of the living God?"*

■ 1 SAMUEL 17:26

When David heard Goliath, he heard all the same words that
the Israelites had heard. He saw the same giant and faced the
same intimidation, but his response was, "How dare you defy the
armies of the living God!"

When the Israelite army heard Goliath, they said, "He is
coming against the army of Israel. David also recognized that
Goliath was coming against the armies of the living God. You can
listen as a mere mortal, or you can listen as a child of the living
God. How you listen will determine your behavior and, therefore,
your results.

David responded, "How dare he do that? How dare he defy
the living God!" David was very vocal about his opinion. In voic-
ing his opinion, David was taking his first jabs at the giant. He
was listening as a child of God.

Then come the side attacks. You make your decision to face
the giant head-on, but then someone comes along and tells you,
"You'll never make it. You might as well give up. You can't do
that!" Someone you respect, who has had a lot of input into your
life, says, "That's a worthless idea, you'll never get healed." That's
a side attack.

David experienced the same types of attacks. When he talked
about the giant, his eye was on the giant, but then came the side
attacks. His oldest brother, Eliab, said:

"Why did you come down here? And with whom have you left those few sheep in the wilderness? I know your pride and the insolence of your heart, for you have come down to see the battle."

■ I SAMUEL 17:28

Eliab basically told him he had no business being there, that he was there only for the entertainment and he should get back to his sheep. Not only did David's family attack him, but Saul came to him and said, "You're just a little boy, and this Goliath has been fighting since he was a little boy."

"You are not able to go against this Philistine to fight with him; for you are but a youth, and he a man of war from his youth."

■ I SAMUEL 17:33

David had great respect for Saul. He was the king.

Don't be shocked when the side attacks come. You have probably already experienced that in your life. When the side attacks come, the key is in not changing your words. When you change your words, that means you've changed who's listening. You're no longer listening as a child of God. As a child of God you are a great person; therefore, you say great words. And great words bring you before great people. That's what happened to David.

David knew his struggle was not in the natural realm, but in the spiritual.

For we do not wrestle against flesh and blood, but against principalities, against powers, against the rulers of the darkness of this age, against the spiritual hosts of wickedness in the heavenly places.

■ EPHESIANS 6:12

FIVE SMOOTH STONES

I want to give you the mechanics for defeating your giants. Just as David picked up five smooth stones from the brook, there are five action points that will help you to defeat your giant.

Then he took his staff in his hand; and he chose for himself five smooth stones from the brook, and put them in a shepherd's bag...and his sling was in his hand. And he drew near to the Philistine.

■ I SAMUEL 17:40

Finally, after all the talk and trying on of armor, David pulls out his slingshot, picks up five smooth stones, and goes out to confront Goliath. Words only go so far, now it's time for confrontation.

Smooth Stone 1: Check your ears.

Remember, who's listening determines who wins. Get rid of the unbelief that's causing you to hear improperly. Jesus said, "Take heed what you hear." (Mark 4:24; Luke 8:18.) Check your ears. If you're hearing as a mere mortal, then get the unbelief out.

Smooth Stone 2: Know that your victory is already settled.

If you've read the book of Revelation, you know that we win! When David faced Goliath, he said, "I killed the lion, I killed the bear, and this uncircumcised Philistine will be no different than the rest of them. I win." The apostle Paul knew his victory was secure and said, "No, despite all these things, overwhelming victory is ours through Christ, who loved us" (Rom. 8:37 NLT).

125

God has already defeated your enemy. You just have to walk it out. Your victory has been settled.

Smooth Stone 3: Reject what distracts you from the real giant.

David's older brother, Eliab, was a distraction. Eliab wasn't the giant. Saul wasn't the giant. The giant is in front of you, and you have to reject the side attacks. Reject the opposition, because you cannot be distracted from the true giant.

Ephesians 6:12 says that you don't wrestle against flesh and blood, but you wrestle against principalities and powers—the devil and his cohorts. That person who is coming against you isn't the real problem. Recognize that it's just an attack from the devil, and don't let it distract you from the real giant.

Smooth Stone 4: Recount your past victories.

David looked back and said, "I killed the lion and I killed the bear. This giant is not going to be a problem." Look back at your life. What has God done for you in the past? He may have rescued you from a horrible life. Maybe God has healed you or provided a financial need, perhaps several needs. Maybe your loved ones or neighbors have come to know Christ. Look back and make a mental list of all the good things God has done for you.

Smooth Stone 5: Specialize in your strengths.

When David came before Saul, Saul tried to put his own armor on him. It was way too heavy, and he could barely move in it. Saul was trying to make him look like a soldier instead of a shepherd.

Be yourself. When I was in Kazakhstan, I could have sat there and thought, *I need to be Marilyn Hickey tonight.* Or, *I need to be*

Kathryn Kuhlman tonight. I need to be Joyce Meyer tonight. No, I needed to be who God made me. God gave you special talents to confront the giants in your life. David's special talent was whirling a slingshot. God used David's strength to kill his giant. Be strong in who God made you to be.

David's story is not unique. The smooth stones that he gathered from the streambed are available for you. These action points set the groundwork, so when David went to face Goliath, Goliath was already dead.

PRAYER FOR WISDOM AND STRENGTH IN DEFEATING YOUR GIANTS

Father God, I thank You that You promise to give me wisdom when I ask. When I face a giant in my life, I need Your wisdom to defeat it. I thank You that I can do all things through Christ who strengthens me, including defeating my giants. Thank You for the gifts and talents You've given me that make me who I am. Strengthen my resolve to rely on You and who You made me to be, not what others think I should be. I thank You that You have already defeated my enemies. In Jesus' name, amen. (James 1:5; Phil. 4:13; Rom. 11:29.)

FIVE SMOOTH STONES YOU CAN USE TO DEFEAT YOUR GIANT

1. *Check your ears.* How are you listening? Are you listening as a child of God or as a mere mortal?

2. *Know that your victory is already settled.* God has already defeated your enemies.

3. *Reject what distracts you from the real giant.* Remember, the real giant is the devil.

4. *Recount your past victories.* What has God brought you through in the past?

5. *Specialize in your strengths.* Use your strengths to defeat your enemy, not the weapons someone else thinks you should use.

QUESTIONS FOR DISCUSSION AND REFLECTION

1. What kinds of giants have you faced in your life? Did you defeat them? How did you defeat them?

2. What is the key to killing giants? How do you typically listen to the giants you encounter?

3. Are there people who try to tell you that you can't defeat the giants? How do you react to them?

4. What are the five smooth stones you can use to defeat your giants?

5. One of the stones is to specialize in your strengths. What are some of your strengths?

6. Another of the stones is to recall your past victories. What are some of the things God has done for you in the past?

7. Are you facing a giant right now? What has God promised you regarding that giant? What steps do you need to take to defeat it?

8. David was able to defeat Goliath on his own terms. What are your giant's terms?

9. Side attacks often come from the people around you, but who is the real enemy?

Section Three:

The Bible Shows You God's Purpose for Your Life

Chapter Eight

Where Do I Begin To Find Purpose for My Life?

You are made in the image of God. Knowing and understanding all that implies is essential to finding your purpose in life. God has given every man three important things: 1) We are all made in His image, 2) We are all unique, and 3) We all contain the breath of the Almighty. The "real" you comes from your heavenly Father. Your ultimate purpose is that everything about you would reflect Christ, but you cannot fulfill that purpose unless you first find your identity in Him.

YOU ARE A MIRACLE

We are not here by mistake. The fact that you have existence is proof of a purposeful God. If you talk to medical experts, they say that the probability of sperm and an egg joining and actually creating a human is miraculous. So the fact that you have life is proof of a purposeful, strategic, intentional God. But how often have you wondered, *Why am I here? Why am I on this planet?*

In this chapter, we are going to discuss why we are here. This is a powerful message. As you read these words, let God make it real to you. It can change both your present and your future, and it can also make your past beneficial.

Now, when we talk about our identity, it's very important for us to understand that who we are is not wrapped up in what we do. Your identity is not limited to what you do—your function—but your identity in Jesus implements your purpose.

In order for you to understand your purpose, you must first understand your identity. You determine the value of many things that you use in life by looking at their purpose. But your real value is found in Jesus. Your identity is in Him. Therefore, before you begin to discover your purpose, you have to first understand who you are. And to understand who you are, you must look at your maker, the One who designed you.

Your car is identified by its manufacturer. Most of the clothes you wear are identified by who made them. Almost any product you can think of is identified by its designer, creator, or manufacturer. In the same way, your identity is determined by who made you.

In Genesis 1:26-27, God says:

"Let Us make man in Our image, according to Our likeness; let them have dominion over the fish of the sea, over the birds of the air, and over the cattle, over all the earth and over every creeping thing that creeps on the earth."

So God created man in His own image; in the image of God He created him; male and female He created them.

According to verse 26, you are made in the image of God. And you are made not only in His image, but also in His likeness. You are made in His image according to His likeness. These are two very interesting words in the Hebrew. *Image* in the Hebrew has the implication of mirror.[1] The connotation then is that man is made as a mirror image of God.

We are also made "according to His likeness." *Likeness* in the Hebrew implies schematic.[2] A schematic is a type of blueprint. You are made according to the blueprint of God. You were designed with God's essential nature. That's who you are! That is your identity!

MADE TO HAVE DOMINION

Now, I want you to understand this. Not only are you made in His image according to His likeness, but if you continue reading in verse 26, it also says that you are made for dominion, to rule over this earth. There is no other creature that God made who was given authority and dominion. Man is unique among God's creation. Every other creature that lives on this earth exists based upon stimuli and response. But you are unique; you are distinct. You have been given authority, dominion, and free will. You are not merely responding to stimuli; you have a choice.

God has given you authority not only to rule over things on the earth but also to rule over yourself. You don't have to just react to things. When someone cuts in front of you on the road, you can decide not to tailgate that person to teach him a lesson. You have a choice. You have been given authority not over other people's cars but over your own behavior. You do not merely respond to outside stimuli. You are made in the image of God and according to His likeness.

Genesis 1 is basically an introduction to Creation— Creation 101, so to speak. But in Genesis 2, God begins to narrow the focus. He begins to specifically identify humanity and describe His interaction with man. God does this very intentionally. He first gives us an overview, but even then He's showing us that our identity is found in Him. Then as you continue into chapter 2, He describes in greater detail how He designed us.

The Lord God formed man of the dust of the ground, and breathed into his nostrils the breath of life; and man became a living being.

■ GENESIS 2:7

What a powerful verse! You may have read that verse before, but I want you to grasp its significance.

Back in Genesis 1, when God is describing the creation of the world and gives us the overview of the creation of man, He uses the Hebrew word *Elohim* for Himself. *Elohim* means "omnipotent, almighty, all-powerful, sovereign, worthy of glory, honor."[3] It implies some distance due to the sheer splendor, majesty, glory, and honor of God. The almighty God who made the universe knit you together.

When we move into Genesis 2 and God begins to describe the fashioning of man, He changes his name from *Elohim*—the Almighty, the Powerful—to *Jehovah*. Jehovah has a different connotation than Elohim. Jehovah is the personal God.[4] He is the God who is hungry for your heart, hungry for relationship with you. He is the God who fashioned you. He knit you together. When He took the dirt in His hand and began to form man, He was very intentional, specific, and personal.

He is both almighty and personal. He made you for relationship with Him. Your identity in Jesus, your relationship with Him, is why you were made. When you grasp that one fact, then your purpose comes naturally because it flows from your identity. Now, continuing in verse 7, it says, "The Lord God" (Jehovah, the Personal God) "formed" man. When you look at the word *form* in the Hebrew, it literally means "to sculpt, hew, shape, mold, fashion."[5] Everything else that He made, He spoke and it existed. When He made humanity, He reached into the dirt and shaped, fashioned, and formed man. He formed man from the dirt, and He made you a masterpiece.

What did God do after He formed man? Look at the next phrase: "He breathed the breath of life and man became a living being."

Until God breathed the breath of life into man, he was just dirt, nothing but a dirt sculpture. As beautiful and amazing as Michelangelo's David is, it's just a sculpture. Michelangelo could not breathe life into his David. The Bible tells us God "breathed into [man's] nostrils."[6] In the Hebrew, the connotation is "animation." God breathed into man's nostrils and animated him, and man became a living being.

Approximately six thousand years later that breath of life has continued and expanded. When you look at yourself in the mirror, remember that within you is God's breath of life. When you see your family and friends, remember that they have been given the breath of life. It has gone on for generations. It has never stopped. You are alive today because you have the breath of the Almighty in you.

The next phrase says, "And man became a living being." Some Bible translations use the word *soul*. However, when these verses were written, the Hebrews had no word for soul. The concept of body, soul, and spirit is a Greek idea. The Hebrews understood only two parts of man: the external, what was observable, and the internal, the invisible but very real part of man.

The portion that God sculpted is the external part of man, but man did not become a living being until God breathed life into him, and that became the internal part of man. The "you" on the inside—the part of yourself that you think of as you—that's the breath of God inside you. When you're alone and quiet, that sense of identity comes from your Creator. You are unique by design.

THREE THINGS GOD HAS GIVEN YOU

There are three things God has given every man.

First, you are made in His image.

When you understand that you are made in the image of God, that you have His essential nature, it takes you from a mere base mammal existence and places you on a higher level.

Second, God has given you distinction.

You are unique. Even if you don't like yourself, God likes you. He's absolutely crazy about you. He designed you so that He could have a relationship with you.

Third, you have the breath of the Almighty within you.

The breath of the Almighty transcends time, people, ethnicity, and language—every imaginable difference among humanity.

When you begin to truly understand that God is your Author, He is your Father, it changes everything. You should have an identity crisis. Get rid of the garbage that limits you and receive your true identity so that you can implement your purpose. Your true Father, your true Creator is not your earthly father, but your heavenly Father.

THREE THINGS GOD HAS GIVEN EVERY MAN

- FIRST, YOU ARE MADE IN HIS IMAGE.

- SECOND, GOD HAS GIVEN YOU DISTINCTION.

- THIRD, YOU HAVE THE BREATH OF THE ALMIGHTY WITHIN YOU.

IDENTITY

Aside from Jesus, we typically receive our identity from one of two places: our family or our performance. Your idea of father-hood may be limited to your earthly father. If your father was an alcoholic, then you may think, *My father was an alcoholic, therefore I am an alcoholic.* Whatever his behaviors or habits, you will tend to believe you will be the same way. And sometimes you may be, but that is only because you haven't chosen to take another path. You do have that choice.

Maybe you think, *I am the stupid person that my parents call me.* Or, *I am the sex addict that my father or my mother was.* You are not; that is not your identity. You have believed a lie, and you're missing your purpose.

If your family life was great and your parents were flawed but loving and forgiving, you may think you cannot function properly outside of their influence. You base everything you are on who your father or mother was.

I remember when I first moved to Kansas City, it was a real struggle for me. The first month or two I cried a lot. I felt like I had left everything in Denver. I left my home, my family, and my name. My sense of identity was wrapped up in all these things. I am thankful for my family, but I realized that I am much more than that. I am not limited by my earthly family, and neither are you.

The second mistake we make in determining our identity is when we base our value on our performance. This is especially easy to do in our society. When we meet someone for the first time, usually the second question we ask is, "What do you do?" Many people are so determined to find their identity apart from their family that they fall into this trap of performance-based identity. They think, *Everything I am is wrapped up in my performance*, on the job or in sports, or in a hobby. The trap is that whatever you do, it will never be enough. You've got to make more money, run faster, write better, and have a more prestigious title.

I know because I am guilty of this as well. I love to perform. I love to achieve. When I achieve a goal, I feel important and valuable. I feel significant. But if that is your only source of identity, you will live a tragic, shallow existence. You were designed to find your identity in Jesus Christ and, therefore, to have a divine purpose.

You are more than your family. You are more than your performance. You are made in His image, according to His likeness. God's identity in you implements your purpose.

I like to use my dad as an example because there are many parallels between him and my heavenly Father. Now, you may think that because both of my parents are in the ministry, I grew up in the perfect family. My father and my mother will be the first to admit to you that they did not do everything correctly. There is no such thing as a perfect family. And while I have some nice parallels between my earthly father and my heavenly Father, I can understand my heavenly Father because of some of the gaps my parents were unable to fill.

If you never had an earthly father, my prayer is that you will see at least a small glimpse of what your heavenly Father is like by reading this book. I pray that God will reveal His fatherhood to you.

My earthly father is a fine-looking young man. He's wonderful. We look alike. I am made in his physical image. But I am not solely the product of my mother and my father, because my identity is not limited to my physical existence. The inside "me" doesn't come from mom and dad. It comes from my heavenly Father. My mom and dad gave me an earthly body and have helped to shape my thinking, but my true self is not from them. It's from my heavenly Father.

I do have some other characteristics that parallel my earthly father. In some respects, we have similar behaviors. I hear myself say something, and I think, *Where did I get that?* Then I realize it's something my father says. My father introduced me to many of the things I like. When I was growing up, my dad and I made hospital visits together.

I also have a keen sense of respect for his authority. I remember one time we were lying on the bed upstairs watching TV. We were just having a nice family time. I was eating an orange and found a seed. There was a trash can on the other side of Dad, so I tried to spit the orange seed over him into the trash can. *PPhhtt.* It landed right on his stomach. Dad thought I was trying to spit on him and got really mad. I was petrified because, as I said, I had (and still have) a keen respect for his authority.

My dad has affirmed my individuality. He loves art. He loves antiques. He doesn't love sports. Sports were kind of irrelevant to him. But when I began to play basketball, he affirmed my individuality by supporting me and coming to my games.

My father didn't do everything right. Like I said, he'd be the first to admit that. But he did a lot of things right. Your dad may be the same way, so there are some good parallels you can see between your earthly father and your heavenly Father.

While your physical existence and some behaviors and characteristics come from your earthly father, the true you comes from your heavenly Father. You're not limited to the context of your earthly father.

And yet, Lord, you are our Father. We are the clay, and you are the potter. We are all formed by your hand.

■ ISAIAH 64:8 NLT

You are the work of His hand. He is your Father. Therefore, your identity in Him implements your purpose. You are made in the image of your heavenly Father. Jeremiah 31:9 says:

They shall come with weeping, and with supplications I will lead them. I will cause them to walk by the rivers of waters, in a straight way in which they shall not stumble; for I am a Father to Israel, and Ephraim is My firstborn.

Your identity in Jesus will implement your purpose when you know that He is your Father and He leads you and guides you. He leads you by rivers of water, in a straight way in which you will not stumble, for He is your *Father.*

Once you have established your identity in Jesus Christ, that you are made in the image of your heavenly Father, your values must line up. Are the things that are important to God important to you? Jesus said, "My food is to do the will of Him who sent Me, and to finish His work" (John 4:34).

Jesus was saying, "What's important to My Father is what drives Me and motivates Me. It's what gives Me purpose." Do we live our lives that way? I want to challenge you: If God is your Father, then you are made in the image of Jesus. You have His identity, and therefore you must reflect His values.

AUTHORITY

Furthermore, in order to fulfill God's purpose for your life, you must surrender to His authority. People who do not respect authority are not respected by others. If you undermine those who are in authority over you, then people will lack respect for you when you are in a position of authority. If you cannot surrender and submit to your heavenly Father, then how can you have dominion?

> *As parents feel for their children, God feels for those who fear him.*
>
> ■ PSALM 103:13 MESSAGE

God has compassion on those who honor, revere, and respect Him.

PROTECTION AND PROVISION

We naturally expect our fathers to protect us and provide for us, and many times they do. But our heavenly Father promises to always protect and provide for us.

A father of the fatherless, a defender of widows, is God in His holy habitation.

■ PSALM 68:5

If you are adopted or you grew up in a single parent family where there was no father, your true father is not your physical father. Your heavenly Father is the truest father you'll ever know. You are made in His image. Your identity is in Him.

Your heavenly Father believes in you even when you are at your worst. He loves you; He affirms you. Isaiah 49:15-16 says:

"Can a woman forget her nursing child, and not have compassion of the son of her womb? Surely they may forget, yet I will not forget you. See, I have inscribed you on the palms of My hands; your walls are continually before Me."

You are carved into your Father's hands. He has never wanted to wash His hands and say, "I'm done with you." You are etched into His hands. You are valuable to Him.

Your heavenly Father has given you eternal life. In Acts 17:28 it says, "In him we live and move and have our being." Your true life is not from your physical father; you have the breath of the Almighty within. In Philippians 2:13 NLT it says, "For God is working in you, giving you the desire to obey him and the power to do what pleases him."

When you have the desire to do something godly, that's your heavenly Father working in you. That's God saying, *Now you're starting to reflect your true nature, your true identity.* When you have the desire to and actually do godly things, that is your heavenly Father working in you. You are being made into His image.

THE PURPOSE

The overriding purpose for your identity in Jesus is found in Second Corinthians 3:18.

We all, with unveiled face, beholding as in a mirror the glory of the Lord, are being transformed into the same image from glory to glory, just as by the Spirit of the Lord.

Your true purpose is that your values, your behavior, your sense of being, your protection—all of those things—are found first in Him so that you reflect His image. I may look like my earthly father, but I am not a mirror of my earthly father. I am a mirror of my heavenly Father.

Look at Psalm 139:13-16 from *The Message*.

Oh yes, you shaped me first inside, then out; you formed me in my mother's womb. I thank you, High God—you're breathtaking! Body and soul, I am marvelously made! I worship in adoration—what a creation! You know me inside and out, you know every bone in my body; You know exactly how I was made, bit by bit, how I was sculpted from nothing into something. Like an open book, you watched me grow from conception to birth; all the stages of my life were spread out before you, the days of my life all prepared before I'd even lived one day.

You are fearfully and wonderfully made. You are made in His image. He is your Father. He is your identity. You are not in the image and the identity of your physical family, nor is your identity based upon them or your performance. Your true identity is found in Jesus. When you understand who you are, then you can fulfill your purpose.

Why are you here? First, because you are made in His image. Second, He made you for relationship with Him. He is the Lord Jehovah; not just omnipotent, Elohim, worthy of power, glory, honor, and praise. He is the personal God who made you so that He could have a relationship with you. If you do not understand who you are, you will never fulfill your purpose. Who you are is totally dependent upon your identity in Jesus.

Prayer That I Would Find My True Identity in Jesus

Heavenly Father, thank You for showing me who I am in Christ. I pray that I would see myself grow more and more into His image and likeness, the way You intended me to be at Creation. I pray that I will grow from glory to glory and reflect Jesus Christ to those around me. Thank You for sending the Holy Spirit to whisper in my ear when I need a reminder of who I really am and whose I am. I belong to You, Lord. You are my loving heavenly Father, and I'm grateful for Your work in my life. In Jesus' name, amen. (2 Cor. 3:18; John 14:26.)

QUESTIONS FOR DISCUSSION AND REFLECTION

1. Where are some of the places people look to find their identity in life? Where do you find yours? Where should you find it?

2. What does it mean to be made in God's "image"?

3. What does it mean to be made according to God's "likeness"?

4. What are three things God has given to every man?

5. Why is it important to submit to God's authority? Have you fully submitted to His authority in your life?

6. What is the purpose of your identity in Christ?

7. How does your identity in Christ relate to your purpose in life?

8. What is the difference between God's names, *Elohim* and *Jehovah?* What do each of these aspects of God mean to you?

9. God "breathed the breath of life" into you. What does that mean? How does it affect who you are?

Chapter Nine

Why Am I Here?

God's Word is the premise for our purpose. It tells us who we are. We are created in God's image, according to His likeness. He breathed into us, and the real person on the inside is the result. This question—"Why am I here?"—must be preceded by the answer to the question of who you are. If the reality of who you are hasn't yet sunk in, I would encourage you to reread the previous chapter before moving on. Understanding *who* you are is absolutely vital to understanding *why* you are here.

God laid out the pattern for our purpose in the book of Genesis. In the story of Abram, we see three areas of purpose that touch each part of our lives: our public life, our private life, and our personal, intimate life. When we cooperate with these purposes by maintaining a commitment to daily Bible reading and prayer and using our talents to further God's kingdom, we begin to fulfill our ultimate purpose.

"Why do I exist? What is my purpose? Why am I here?" I would guess we all struggle with that sense of unfulfilled destiny from time to time. I think every one of us at some point wishes we would get a message every day like the special agents in the show *Mission Impossible*.

"Your mission today, should you choose to accept it is...."

Of course, it would spell out for you in specific detail your goals and objectives for the day. It might even supply the names of people who might help you and list all the supplies you might need.

However, God does not lead us that way, for "His ways are higher than our ways and His thoughts higher than our thoughts." (Isaiah 55:9.) He leads us first and foremost through His Word. That's why I emphasized the importance of daily Bible reading and memorization in the first section of this book. Let me say again that knowing the Word of God is essential to knowing and understanding your purpose. His Word is the premise for your purpose.

EAT, WORK, SLEEP

I would propose that many of us, maybe even today, have said, "Is my life supposed to be only eating, working, and sleeping? Is this all there is?" Eat, work, sleep; eat, work, sleep. Over and over.

We feel like we're caught on this endless treadmill. But why? "Is that really what I was made for? Am I merely a robot? I wake up every morning. At this certain time, I do this. Next I do this, then that," and so on.

Most of us have a daily routine. Mine goes something like this: I wake up, pull myself together, grab a cup of coffee. Sit down and read my Bible, get myself ready, go to work, then come home, eat, sleep, and do the same thing the next morning. Your routine may be similar. But is that really why we were born? Is that our purpose? Is that why we exist? God wants to identify for you why you exist. What is your purpose? Do you have a divine purpose beyond eating, working, and sleeping? The answer is *yes!*

God has purpose for you beyond your daily routine. A common mistake we make in life is to try and carve out our own purpose. We try to make something happen. We try to feel significant in what we're doing. We try to force our purpose to manifest itself. I want to revolutionize your thinking: God already has a purpose for you. You don't have to sweat and strain to develop your own purpose in life. You merely need to receive it from God and cooperate with Him to fulfill your purpose. God has a wonderful purpose for you. You are not a mistake. You are here by divine design.

THREE DISTINCT PURPOSES

In the Word of God, we find three distinct purposes God has ordained for each one of us. He did not write His purpose for you at the end of the Bible or as an afterthought. He has known you and had a plan for your life from the very foundations of the earth. (Eph. 1:4.) He wrote His purpose for you in the Bible at the very beginning in Genesis, because God knew the first and deepest need of your soul would be to know who you are and why you are here.

In Genesis, God addresses our purposes: "Why do I exist?" I love how He addresses this issue because He shows us perfectly through Abram. We know him better as Abraham, of course, but God gave him purpose and spoke these things into Abram's life before his name was changed.

Purpose 1: Becoming part of the kingdom of God (public life)

We will find the first purpose God gave Abram in Genesis 12:1-3.

> *Now the Lord had said to Abram: "Get out of your country, from your [kindred] and from your father's house, to a land that I will show you. I will make you a great nation; I will bless you and make your name great; and you shall be a blessing. I will bless those who bless you, and I will curse him who curses you; and in you all the families of the earth shall be blessed."*

This is the first time that God speaks with Abram. In the first verse, God told him, "I want you to leave your country and go into a land I will show you." Then He continues, "I will make you a great nation."

The first purpose for our life addresses becoming a part of the kingdom of God, the nation of God. When God spoke this to Abram, He was not only speaking to Abram but He was also speaking to us. We are called to be a part of His kingdom on this earth. Now, how does that work itself out in your life? How do you become a part of His kingdom and make a contribution?

In order to answer that, let me give you three fundamental components of nationhood. The first component is having an actual land, a geography. The second component deals with people. And the third component of nationhood deals with authority and government. We will look at each of these components in relation to each of God's purposes being fulfilled in our lives.

We can see that in relation to God's first purpose, He called Abram out and gave him a new land. You were put in your land, the geographic location where you live, by divine design.

In Acts 17:26-27 it says:

"He has made from one blood every nation of men to dwell on all the face of the earth, and has determined their preappointed times and the boundaries of their habitation. So that they should seek the Lord, in the hope that they might grope for Him and find Him, though He is not far from each one of us."

It is not an accident that you live in your country, state or province, city or town, village or neighborhood. You live where you do by God's divine purpose.

Purpose 2: To Grow God's Family (personal life)

The second purpose God has for you is to grow His family. His family means your immediate, natural family in the home, but it also extends to your church family, the family of God. Notice it says in Genesis 13:16, "I will make your descendants as the dust of the earth." That doesn't mean God is grinding His descendants down; He's speaking of numbers. The following verse says, "So that if a man could count the number of the dust of the earth, then your descendants also could be numbered."

God never intended for His family to be a small, exclusive, elite group. God's purpose is for a massive family. However,

God not only wants increase in His family, but He also wants to fulfill His purpose in your personal family. Now let's look at how this actually applies to our lives by looking at each of the two applications.

Application 1: How do we cooperate with God's purpose in growing our personal family?

How do you relate to your family members? How do you interact with your husband or wife, with your kids? How do you interact with your parents, your brother, your sister? God's purpose is for your family interactions to be godly. When we operate with this purpose, we're saying, "Yes, I agree. Father God, I will cooperate with Your purpose in my personal family."

Application 2: How do we cooperate with God's purpose in growing our church family?

This application deals with growing the family of God. Another name for the family of God is "church." God's purpose for us as members of our church family is to help grow His church—His family. So practically speaking, how do we receive His purpose in this context and cooperate with that?

In our church, one of the ways we do that is by being involved in "cells," or small groups. A cell is not only for discipling and growing people, receiving purpose, and cooperating with purpose but also to reach out and evangelize. It's a twofold purpose. It is a vital part of how we grow our church family.

Your church may have something different. It may be Sunday school classes, Bible study groups, or simply areas where you can volunteer in the church. The simplest yet most effective way to walk out this purpose in your life is to get involved in your church, the family of God. Do something–join the choir, serve as an usher, or help in the nursery. Every church has some area where you can "put your hand to the plow" and do your part in helping that church family grow.

THINGS YOU CAN DO TO HELP GROW YOUR CHURCH FAMILY

- Sing in the choir
- Play an instrument
- Serve as a greeter
- Serve as an usher
- Volunteer in the office
- Help count the offering
- Serve as a security volunteer
- Serve as a parking lot attendant
- Work in the nursery
- Work in the preschool area
- Work in the children's church
- Write, edit, or typeset the church bulletin or newsletter
- Volunteer in the audio/visual department
- Volunteer in the computer department
- Teach a small group

- Handle administrative duties for a small group

- Organize meals for new parents, those who've had a death in the family, or those who are ill

- Visit people in the hospital

- Serve as a counselor

- Serve in the prayer room

- Pray!

This list could go on and on. Take an inventory of your skills. Write down everything you can think of that you know how to do, even things you take for granted. Not everyone has the same skills. Think of creative ways you can use those skills to help your church. Call the pastor or someone on staff and go over your list with them. They can probably think of several areas where your skills would be a great asset to the church.

God has given you special talents and gifts not only for your own benefit but also for your church family. Maybe you have good administrative skills. You're good at organizing and managing. Maybe your talent is hospitality. You tend to make people feel welcome.

There are as many different talents and skills as there are people in the world, but let me give you a couple of examples of how people are using their skills and talents to help grow our church.

One woman in our church is a recruiter for colleges and universities. She's one of the best in the nation. Universities all over the country ask her to come and help them. She donated some of her time and her gifts to help us grow our Bible school. Now that's a phenomenal way to help grow the family.

Sometimes we unintentionally limit ourselves. We think, *The only way I can help grow my church family is through being an usher or a greeter.* And, yes, those are great ways to help grow the family, but there are ways you may not have thought about before. Start thinking "out of the box." Think of the skills and talents you use at work, or the talents you use in running your home, managing your finances, or raising your children. Your church family can benefit from everything that you use in your everyday life. You may have skills that you don't even consider particularly useful because they're so second nature, such as organizing, cooking, or being a good listener. All those things have tremendous value and can help your church family grow.

There is another person in our church who has great talent with computers. Two or three times a month she comes in and volunteers in our Network Administration Department. She's helping us immensely by teaching us how to streamline our work. So she is growing her church family with her talents.

Look at the chart on pgs. 157-158 and circle the talents you possess. If you can think of something you don't see listed, write it down. You have not been given gifts and skills indiscriminately, but God has been very strategic and purposeful about it. Your gifts and talents are not random; they are very purposeful. God gave them to you to fulfill His purpose. Now the question is, Will you cooperate with Him? I challenge you to look at your list of talents and see where you can put them to good use in your church.

The second component of nationhood relates to God's second purpose for your life. You are called to be a catalyst for building the nation, or the kingdom of God, on this earth. The practical application of this is that we are called to advance God's kingdom where we live and where we work in our communities, in our neighborhoods, in our churches, and in our families. I think that sometimes as Christians we have the misconception that promoting the kingdom of God is something only preachers do. But you're missing your divine purpose if you're not working to advance the kingdom of God. Again, all we must do to walk this out is receive this purpose from God by saying, "Okay, I will cooperate with You in advancing Your kingdom today."

"Okay," you say. "I receive it and will cooperate with God, but what do I *do*?" What about the people you work with? What about your neighbors? We sometimes think we have to go out and evangelize and turn into somebody that we're not. But God says,

It's very simple. If you'll receive My purpose, if you'll cooperate with Me, I'll open the opportunities for you to fulfill your purpose.

It's merely an issue of saying, "Yes, I receive Your purpose. Yes, I will cooperate with You." Then watch Him open the doors to fulfilling your purpose. God does this in many, many different ways. It's not about just talking to people specifically about Jesus, but also simple things such as being nice. It's about being nice even if you work in a cubicle.

Many of us get in our little cubes and stay focused on our work, but there are people all around us. And because they're in a cube as well, sometimes it seems as if they're not there. However, there are some very simple ways you can minister to those around you. You don't have to beat them over the head with Jesus; show them Jesus. Sometimes it's as simple as being kind to the person who works in the cubicle next to you and bringing them a cup of coffee or a glass of water.

There are simple things you can do to reflect God's purpose in your life and advance His kingdom. It's simply a question of you cooperating with Him. God wants us to advance His kingdom in our life through people.

Purpose 3: To Have a Relationship With God (personal life)

The third purpose God has for us is really the most important. God saved the best for last. Just to review, our first purpose is more on a public level, the second is more private, but the third purpose is personal. He touches our most intimate, personal relationship—our relationship with Him.

> [Abram] *believed in the Lord, and He accounted it to him for*
> *righteousness. Then He said to him, "I am the Lord, who*
> *brought you out of Ur of the Chaldeans, to give you this land to*
> *inherit it."*

■ GENESIS 15:6,7

In these verses, God describes what He means by having a
relationship with Him. We see how He works this out with
Abram. Very few of us in the twenty-first century truly understand what the word *covenant* means. Our nearest synonym to
that is *contract,* but even some contracts have lost part of their
significance over the years. In our world, contracts, agreements,
and promises are broken all the time. Many times people don't
keep their word, and they think of very little other than the possible legal consequences before choosing to break a contract.
Marriage is a covenant, and it's obvious from the divorce rate
that most people don't understand the significance of that
covenant. A covenant has a lot more to it than being simply a
promise or an agreement.

A covenant with God has a much deeper meaning than a
contract between men. In essence, God is establishing an everlasting relationship with Abram. God tells Abram, "I want you to
go and get five different animals." He lists them and then says,
"And I want you to cut them in half."(Gen. 15.)

That sounds pretty disgusting. Remember when you had to
dissect something in biology class in high school? Well, that was-
n't so bad because you had formaldehyde. It was probably just the
smell that got to you. But this is not Biology 101. This is Life 101.

God tells Abram, "Go get live animals; slice them in half because I want to have a covenant with you."

Why did he have to slice the animals in half? Well, when Abram split the animals in half, God was in essence saying, "I am initiating a relationship with you. I am coming into promise, into a covenant." He was saying, "If I break this covenant with you, this is what will happen to Me." That's covenant. God made you for a relationship with Him. For Him to break that relationship with you, He would be splitting Himself in half. God was saying, "Abram, we are now one. If I break my promise to you, I'm splitting Myself in two." God made you for relationship with Him. That's the third purpose for your life.

THREE PURPOSES GOD HAS FOR EVERY BELIEVER

PURPOSE 1: TO BECOME PART OF THE KINGDOM OF GOD (PUBLIC LIFE)

PURPOSE 2: TO GROW GOD'S FAMILY—BOTH IN THE HOME AND CHURCH (PRIVATE LIFE)

PURPOSE 3: TO HAVE A RELATIONSHIP WITH GOD (PERSONAL LIFE)

Now, how do I cooperate with this purpose in my daily life? The way I cooperate with it is very simple. It is through being in the Word every day. Your daily Bible reading and prayer time is not intended to be a daily regimen but an ongoing relationship. So when you come to the Word of God, you come to it not because you *have* to read your Bible every day or else someone is going to hound you about it at church, but because you're growing in your relationship with God.

The third component of nationhood deals with authority and government. That seems broad in relationship to this personal, intimate purpose for our lives, but we can experience this purpose only by submitting to God's authority. The way this works itself out in our lives is through our surrendering to God's lordship. And remember, this is the aspect of our purpose that relates to our inner life, our intimate relationship with God. That one relationship affects and spills over into both our private and public lives.

When it comes to dealing with authority, the issue is this: Will we let God rule in us? Will we be people of integrity? Will we be loyal? Will we live a life of moral character? Will we be honorable? Will we be people of our word? The questions we should ask ourselves are these: "Will I cooperate with God's purpose? Will I cooperate with God's purpose to advance His kingdom in my neighborhood, in my family, with my friends, in my workplace, in my community, and in my school? Will I cooperate with God and say, 'Yes, God, I receive Your purpose. Father, open the doors, open the possibilities'?" Because when you ask Him, He will.

If we start to think, *I have to do it, I have to do it, I have to do it,* then our perception is faulty. God wants to give you purpose; you don't have to "do" anything but say, "Yes, I receive." And then He opens the doors. It's a matter of your making a commitment. Will you commit to cooperating with God's purpose in your life?

You may have made that commitment before. Maybe you were in church and you committed with all of your heart to receive and cooperate with God's purpose in your life, but what happened the next day when you got to work and your cube-mate was cranky? Or when somebody sent you a mean E-mail? You felt like everywhere you turned, you got a slap in the face. How did your commitment fare outside of church, in the face of opposition? It's an opportunity for you to be determined to cooperate with God's purpose in your life.

These are very practical ways that we cooperate with God's purpose: by showing love and being surrendered to His authority in our lives.

THE THREE COMPONENTS OF NATIONHOOD

1. HAVING AN ACTUAL LAND, A GEOGRAPHY

2. HAVING A PEOPLE

3. SUBMITTING TO AUTHORITY

So why are we here? We are here to receive God's purposes for our life and to cooperate with them in our daily life. Relationship with God penetrates our purpose. It penetrates all of the purposes we discussed in this chapter.

When you study Genesis 12 and look at the terminology God uses when He talks with Abram, you'll find that God does not call Himself the Almighty. He uses the term "Jehovah," the personal God. He is not remote; He is personal. He is right there beside us. In working out His kingdom through us, when we are cooperating with that purpose, we are walking in relationship with Him, the Father of relationship.

Building God's kingdom, growing God's family, and walking in covenant relationship with God doesn't mean you have to become a minister or a preacher. It means you have to do the best you can at what God has given you to do. If you have the talent to make money, then do it the best you can and use that talent to sow into God's kingdom. If you have been given administrative skills or people skills, use those skills to the best of your ability and incorporate them into your church and into the world around you.

This relationship with God is the premise for our purpose. If we do not have a relationship with God, then how can we grow in our families? How can we grow personally? How can we fulfill our purpose? How can we cooperate with God if we do not have a relationship with Him? We are purpose-driven people—not random, not accidental, but purposeful. Our purpose is to build His kingdom, to grow our families, and to have a relationship with

God; that is why we exist. And when we cooperate with that purpose, our life will be fuller than we could ever imagine.

Prayer Asking God To Show You How To Cooperate Daily With the Purposes Revealed in His Word

Heavenly Father, I thank You that, like Abram, I am in covenant with You through Jesus. Thank You for revealing Your purpose for my life through Your Word, and I thank You for showing me in even greater detail how those purposes specifically apply to my life. Thank You for sending the Holy Spirit to be my teacher and lead me into all truth. I am determined to do Your will, Lord. Thank You for strengthening me to walk out Your plan for my life. In Jesus' name, amen. (Luke 22:20.)

QUESTIONS FOR DISCUSSION AND REFLECTION

1. Where can you find the foundation for your purpose in life?

2. Before you tackle the issue of "why" you're here, you must know "who" you are. Who are you?

3. What are the three primary purposes God has for your life?

4. How can you help your church family grow? How can you help your immediate family grow?

5. What are some of the ways you can cooperate with God's purposes in your daily life?

6. What is the first component of nationhood, and how does it relate to God's first purpose for your life?

7. What is the second component of nationhood, and how does it relate to God's second purpose for your life?

8. What is the third component of nationhood, and how does it relate to God's third purpose for your life?

9. Which of these purposes is most important and has a direct effect on the others?

Chapter Ten

How Do I Recognize and Combat the Lies That Can Extinguish My Purpose?

Firstborn sons, particularly in the nation of Israel, have a special position in life. In the lives of three firstborn sons of the Old Testament, we will see three lies that can snuff out our purpose in life. When we recognize these lies and learn the opposing truth from God's Word, our flame of purpose can be reignited.

In the previous chapters we've discussed who we are and why we are here. We've learned that before we know what our purpose is, we have to know who we are, and we have to address our identity. We learned that our identity is in Christ. Then we were able to tackle the question, "Why do I exist?"

Are we here on this planet for thousands and thousands of days just to get up every morning, drink coffee, go to work, eat, and then repeat that cycle? Eat, work, sleep; eat, work, sleep; eat, work, sleep; eat, work, sleep. Is that the only reason we exist? Is that our purpose? We learned that the answer is no. We were made for much more than that.

God showed us through Genesis 12, 13, and 15 that our purpose is to build the kingdom of God through our talents, our gifts, our abilities, and our external life—the life around us. God also showed us in Genesis 13 that we are to build His family. We learned that we're to be involved in church and to grow His strength in our families at home and in church. He wants to have His authority rule and reign in our home life with our family members.

Our third purpose is for a relationship with God. Those are the three reasons that we exist, and we work those reasons out in the various capacities of our lives. But I would propose to you that most of us have had our purpose extinguished from time to time. There are things that we have believed—lies—that have tried to extinguish the purpose in our lives.

My goal in this chapter is to expose those lies so that you can fulfill God's purpose for your life. You don't have to live an extinguished, purposeless life. As you read this chapter, God is going to reignite some of those purposes in your life. Maybe even some things that you didn't realize had been extinguished.

By now I'm sure you're aware that you were made for a specific purpose. God has a plan for your life. The challenge is to keep pursuing your purpose. In order to do that, you cannot believe the lies that the devil brings to try and snuff out your purpose. God has a purpose and plan for you. You need to be aware of and watch for these lies so you're not living a purposeless life.

It's very easy to identify these lies once you are aware of them, because they have been perpetuated since the dawn of man. They're not new; they're not reinvented. They may come in different clothes, but they're still the same old lies. The way we can learn and understand these lies is by looking at various individuals in Genesis who let their purpose be extinguished because they believed a lie.

FIRSTBORN SONS

We'll look at the firstborn sons of very key people of the Old Testament. You may be a firstborn son yourself, or you may have a firstborn son. Firstborn sons are very key, vital family members. There's a unique identity, a unique role, a unique purpose for firstborn sons.

In most cases, we see that a firstborn son has a special relationship with his father. When you see a father with his firstborn son, the first thing you may notice is how he swells up with pride when he says, "That's my son." There's often a unique and distinct, sweet relationship between a firstborn son and his father.

Another typical characteristic of firstborn sons is their strategic position in the family. They're oftentimes chosen to lead the families. We see in Genesis, especially, that they were called upon by God to build the nation of Israel. Firstborn sons were very, very key. They had a keen and obvious purpose. People looked at them and said, "Oh, you're the firstborn. Your purpose is...."

However, we're going to look in the book of Genesis at three firstborn sons who allowed their purpose to be extinguished. And they did this by believing a lie.

REUBEN

Lie 1: Doing the wrong thing is worse than doing nothing.

Reuben was the firstborn son of Jacob. He was supposed to lead his family, to secure them in the nation, and he was supposed to have a keen, distinct relationship with his father.

But Reuben believed a lie. He believed the lie that doing the wrong thing is worse than not doing anything. What do I mean by that? Sometimes we believe that it's better for us not to do anything than to do the wrong thing. So we do nothing. We "wait and see" because we don't want to do the wrong thing; therefore, we do nothing. This was the lie Reuben believed.

We see an example of this in World War II. In Germany there were millions and millions of Germans, and there were several million Jews as well. Several thousand Germans stood up during Word War II and said that what was happening to the Jews was wrong. However, there were millions more Germans who believed it was wrong but said and did nothing, which contributed to the deaths of so many people. That is the lie: It's better to do nothing than to do the wrong thing.

So how does this lie extinguish your purpose? We can see a very clear example of this in Reuben's life. In Genesis 34, this is one of the first examples where Reuben believed the lie.

Reuben's purpose was to be a leader in his family and to protect and grow his family in the nation of Israel. Reuben had a sister named Dinah who was raped by a man named Hamar, who lived in a nearby village. He deeply loved Dinah, and even after he raped her, he still wanted to marry her. So he went to Jacob and his family and said, "I want to marry Dinah. Whatever it takes, I'll do it."

The family discussed it, and they went back to Hamar and said, "Okay, you can marry her if all of the males in your city agree to become circumcised, because for us this is covenant, a very solemn agreement."

So Hamar said, "No problem. We'll do that." Then he went back to his village, and all of the males there went through the process of circumcision. Well, if you look at verse 25, Simeon and Levi went into Hamar's city while the men were still weak from being circumcised and killed every man.

Now you may ask, "What does that have to do with Reuben?" Well, where is he? He's supposed to be their leader, one of the heads of the family. He should be helping to build and protect the nation of Israel, but he's nowhere to be found. He is absent from this discussion.

The result is this. In Genesis 34:30, Jacob says to Simeon and Levi, "You have troubled me by making me obnoxious among the inhabitants of this land. You have jeopardized this family in this land." Where's Reuben? He missed his purpose by his absence.

We believe the lie when we say, "Oh, it's okay for me not to talk to someone at work. It's okay for me to go along with any problems with morality at work or in my nation." We believe the lie that inactivity is acceptable, but the truth is that inactivity extinguishes purpose. Possibly doing the wrong thing with the right motive is better than standing by and doing nothing at all.

Another major example where Reuben's inactivity, his absence, is very clear is in relation to Joseph's sale into slavery. If you remember this story, Joseph came along looking for his brothers, and they spotted him from a distance. They said, "Oh, there's the jerk. Let's kill him." They hated him.

So they saw Joseph coming and began to plot and plan. Reuben, to his credit, stands up and says, "Throw him in this pit." But in the back of his mind he's thinking, *I'll come and get him and then take him to Dad and he'll be safe.* However, we know that Reuben did not make it back to rescue Joseph from being sold into slavery. Reuben was not even there to protect him.

It says in Genesis 37:29, "Then Rueben returned to the pit." He was absent. How could he return if he was already there? He wasn't there; he was absent.

Just as Reuben did, we so often think, *Well, it's okay for me to be absent, to be distant, to be inactive...no one will notice anyway.* We believe the lie and therefore extinguish our purpose.

We can see from Reuben's life that inactivity is a sad thing when we discuss it in relation to purpose. Imagine you are a candle. What is the purpose of a candle? To give light. If it's not lit, it is not doing what it was made to do. Right? But when you light it, it begins to fulfill its purpose.

Our purpose is to bring light, but if we exclude or isolate ourselves, we are inactive and we extinguish our purpose. When we believe the lie that it's okay to be inactive, we suffocate the purpose for which God made us.

Reuben's purpose was to help build the nation of Israel. He was to exercise moral authority, protect the land, and grow his family, but his lack of action suffocated his purpose.

Lie 2: Immediate gratification equals a purposeful life.

Now let's look at the second lie. The second lie says that immediate gratification equals a purposeful life. What do I mean by that? Well, the perfect example that we see in the Bible is Esau, who was the firstborn of Isaac. Because he was the firstborn, naturally, he was supposed to lead the family, build a nation, and have a distinct, unique relationship with his father. But when you study his life, you will discover that he believed meeting the flesh's appetites and desires was equally as fulfilling as living the purpose-filled life.

Esau

Let's look at Genesis 25:30-34.

And Esau said to Jacob, "Please feed me with that same red stew, for I am weary." Therefore his name was called Edom. But Jacob said, "Sell me your birthright as of this day." And Esau said, "Look, I am about to die; so what profit shall this birthright be to me?" Then Jacob said, "Swear to me as of this day." So he swore to him, and sold his birthright to Jacob. And Jacob gave Esau bread and stew of lentils; then he ate and drank, arose, and went his way. Thus Esau despised his birthright.

Esau has been out hunting and killing game. In the meantime, Jacob was back at the ranch, minding the stew. Soon Esau comes running in, shouting, "I'm famished! I'm so hungry. Give me food!"

Jacob, very cleverly says, "What's it worth to you?"

"Anything. I want food!"

So Jacob says, "Well, how about your birthright?"

"Whatever it takes."

Esau's birthright was the right to the privileges and inheritance of the firstborn. At the time, Esau's flesh cried so loudly for sustenance that he believed a bowl of soup was more valuable than his birthright. He believed the lie that his immediate hunger, his immediate need, was equal to or more important than his divine purpose.

These lies are not new lies. We see them every day. Our family is not comprised of only our parents, our siblings, or our husband or wife, but it is also our family in our church. We too often exchange our natural appetites for our purpose in the larger family of God.

How is this manifest? Well, very simply. What about when our children have soccer on Sunday morning? We say, "Oh, sorry, gotta take the kids to soccer." What about when we're tired and we want to sleep in on Sunday morning? "Oh, it's more important for me to get my sleep than to be involved in my church family." That's the lie, and it is threatening to extinguish your purpose.

It's very easy to let these things slip in. We think buying a new pair of shoes is so much more fulfilling than paying our tithe. We exchange fleshly appetites for purpose. As a believer, you are called to embrace the purpose of the body of Christ. That seems like an enormous task, but the place to start is by helping to fulfill the purpose of your church family.

The stated purpose of our church is to grow in our individual families, grow in the church as a family, and grow in Bible study. Our tendency is to fill our lives with so many *things* that we exchange purpose for natural appetites and desires. However, that doesn't mean there is no place for other "natural" things in our lives. There is a place of balance in this.

I played basketball growing up and loved it. But I did not miss church on Sunday morning to play basketball. Yes, my parents were the pastors, but even if they hadn't been, we still would not have missed church for basketball.

I want to challenge you to identify the things in your life that are fleshly appetites, things that you think are fulfilling in your life, but you've exchanged your true purpose in God to pursue those things.

Remember the candle? Here's what happens. We fill our lives with this and that, and we get so much activity going in our lives that we create too much air and it blows out the candle. The candle needs air to fuel its flame, but too much air extinguishes it, snuffs it out. We do need these things, but in balance. We cannot believe the lie that our natural appetites are equally as fulfilling as our divine purpose in family and church.

Lie 3: Sin is greater than my ability to say no.

The third lie says that sin is greater than my ability to say no. When we believe this lie, we think, *I cannot master sin. It's too powerful for me.* We believe that we are slaves to sin. We can see the belief of this lie demonstrated in the life of Cain.

CAIN

Cain was the firstborn of Adam. One of his distinct and unique purposes was to have a relationship with Adam. He was supposed to be his dad's buddy, hanging out, connected, tight. But if you recall, he made an offering from his vegetables and fruits, and his brother Abel made an offering from livestock. Abel's offering was accepted by God, but Cain's offering was not. Cain was very upset. So upset, in fact, that he had some very negative thoughts toward his brother. But God catches him. He hooks Cain and says, "Wait."

> *"If you do well, will you not be accepted? And if you do not do well, sin lies at the door. And its desire is for you, but you should rule over it."*

■ GENESIS 4:7

The truth is that Cain was made in the image of God. He was created to have dominion. (Gen. 1:26.) Cain chose not to do what was right and killed his brother, Abel.

In Romans 6:6 NLT it says:

Our old sinful selves were crucified with Christ so that sin might lose its power in our lives. We are no longer slaves to sin.

And Romans 6:14 NLT says:

Sin is no longer your master, for you are no longer subject to the law, which enslaves you to sin. Instead, you are free by God's grace.

Usually there are sins in our lives that we constantly struggle with. We often feel we have to give in to them. The pull seems too powerful for us. It may be pornography, addiction, gossip, pride, shame, or thoughts of being unworthy. But none of those things can rule over you. When you believe the lie that you cannot master sin, then you extinguish your purpose.

You are not a shameful person. You are wonderfully and beautifully made. Whatever has happened to you, shame does not have to master you. Whatever has happened to you, whatever you have done, you are worthy because of what Jesus did, not because of your own actions. You do not have to bow to pornography. You do not have to bow to alcoholism. You were created to have dominion. You are not the slave.

THREE LIES THAT EXTINGUISH PURPOSE

LIE 1: DOING THE WRONG THING IS WORSE THAN DOING NOTHING.

LIE 2: IMMEDIATE GRATIFICATION EQUALS A PURPOSEFUL LIFE.

LIE 3: SIN IS GREATER THAN MY ABILITY TO SAY NO.

This lie says, *I was not made in the image of God, I was not made to rule, but rather to be ruled.* This lie says, *I'm not a candle.* This lie snips the wick and says, *I'm just a piece of wax.* This lie says, *I have no dominion, I have no mastery, and I have no authority.* Once we believe that lie, it extinguishes our purpose. The candle is still candle. It doesn't matter that the wick has been snipped. The wick is still there, and it still has the potential to burn.

After reading this, you may recognize one area, or several areas, in your life where you have allowed one or more of these lies to extinguish your purpose. All is not lost. You are not without hope. The flame of the Holy Spirit can reignite your purpose when you recognize the lies, repent of them, and rededicate yourself to moving on with your divine purpose.

Below you will find three prayers, one corresponding to each of the three purposes, that extinguish the lies we've discussed in this chapter. You may feel it necessary to pray only one or two, or perhaps you'll feel led to pray all three.

If your purpose has been extinguished by inactivity, whether you believed a lie or behaved in a wrong way, we pray that God will reignite your candle and show you the things that He would have you do and help you get on with His purposes for your life.

PRAYER OF REPENTANCE FROM BELIEVING THE LIE OF INACTIVITY

Heavenly Father, I thank You that the lie of doing nothing is better than doing the wrong thing has been exposed in my life. I repent from believing that lie, and I choose to embrace Your purpose for my life. I thank You that You are faithful and just, and You forgive me and cleanse me from my sin. Thank You, Father, that the Holy Spirit will reignite the flame in my heart. I pray that it would burn brighter than ever as I walk out Your plan for my life. In Jesus' name, amen. (1 John 1:9.)

PRAYER OF REPENTANCE FROM BELIEVING THE LIE OF IMMEDIATE GRATIFICATION

Father God, I thank You for Your forgiveness. Thank You for cleansing me and making me new. Lord, I thank You for the Holy Spirit who will lead me into all truth. Thank You that He walks alongside me and warns me when I am tempted to believe this lie. Teach me to wait on You, Lord. I choose to be patient with Your plans and purposes for my life, knowing that You are faithful to complete the work You've begun in me. In Jesus' name, amen. (Ps. 51:10-11; John 14:26; Phil. 1:6.)

PRAYER OF REPENTANCE FROM BELIEVING THE LIE THAT SIN CAN CONTROL ME

Heavenly Father, I repent. I know from Your Word that sin no longer has control over me. My freedom was bought with the blood of Jesus. His blood cleanses me from my sin. I repent for my sins, and I thank You that You make me new. Create in me a clean heart and renew a right spirit in me, Lord. Thank You for restoring to me the joy

of Your salvation. Sin no longer masters me; I am free in Jesus Christ. In His name, amen. (Rom. 6:6,14; 1 John 1:7; Ps. 51:10,11; Ps. 51:12; John 8:36.)

Remember, you are made in the image of God and were created to have dominion. You were made for a specific purpose. The potential is there, but the question is, Will you believe God or the lie?

QUESTIONS FOR DISCUSSION AND REFLECTION

1. Why are firstborn sons considered to be special?

2. How did Reuben allow his purpose to be extinguished? Which lie did he believe? Have you ever believed this lie?

3. How did Esau allow his purpose to be extinguished? Which lie did he believe? Have you ever believed this lie?

4. How did Cain allow His purpose to be extinguished? Which lie did he believe? Have you ever believed this lie?

5. How have you been set free from believing these lies? What can you do to make sure your purpose isn't extinguished, or how can you reignite your purpose?

Appendix

BIBLE READING PLAN

WEEK 1

MONDAY	Genesis 1-2; Matthew 1
TUESDAY	Genesis 3-4; Matthew 2
WEDNESDAY	Genesis 5-6; Matthew 3
THURSDAY	Genesis 7-8; Matthew 4
FRIDAY	Genesis 9-10; Matthew 5
SATURDAY	Genesis 11-12; Matthew 6
SUNDAY	Genesis 13-15; Matthew 7-8

WEEK 2

MONDAY	Genesis 16-17; Matthew 9
TUESDAY	Genesis 18-19; Matthew 10
WEDNESDAY	Genesis 20-21; Matthew 11
THURSDAY	Genesis 22-23; Matthew 12
FRIDAY	Genesis 24-25; Matthew 13
SATURDAY	Genesis 26-27; Matthew 14
SUNDAY	Genesis 28-30; Matthew 15-16

WEEK 3

MONDAY	Genesis 31-32; Matthew 17
TUESDAY	Genesis 33-34; Matthew 18
WEDNESDAY	Genesis 35-36; Matthew 19
THURSDAY	Genesis 37-38; Matthew 20
FRIDAY	Genesis 39-40; Matthew 21
SATURDAY	Genesis 41-42; Matthew 22
SUNDAY	Genesis 43-45; Matthew 23-24

WEEK 4

MONDAY	Genesis 46-47; Matthew 25
TUESDAY	Genesis 48-49; Matthew 26
WEDNESDAY	Genesis 50-Exodus 1; Matthew 27
THURSDAY	Exodus 2-3; Matthew 28
FRIDAY	Exodus 4-5; Mark 1
SATURDAY	Exodus 6-7; Mark 2
SUNDAY	Exodus 8-10; Mark 3-4

WEEK 5

MONDAY	Exodus 11-12; Mark 5
TUESDAY	Exodus 13-14; Mark 6
WEDNESDAY	Exodus 15-16; Mark 7
THURSDAY	Exodus 17-18; Mark 8
FRIDAY	Exodus 19-20; Mark 9
SATURDAY	Exodus 21-22; Mark 10
SUNDAY	Exodus 23-25; Mark 11-12

WEEK 6

MONDAY	Exodus 26-27; Luke 1
TUESDAY	Exodus 28-29; Luke 2
WEDNESDAY	Exodus 30-31; Luke 3
THURSDAY	Exodus 32-33; Luke 4
FRIDAY	Exodus 34-35; Luke 5
SATURDAY	Exodus 36-37; Luke 6
SUNDAY	Exodus 38-40; Luke 7-8

WEEK 7

MONDAY	Leviticus 1-2; Luke 9
TUESDAY	Leviticus 3-4; Luke 10
WEDNESDAY	Leviticus 5-6; Luke 11
THURSDAY	Leviticus 7-8; Luke 12
FRIDAY	Leviticus 9-10; Luke 13
SATURDAY	Leviticus 11-12; Luke 14
SUNDAY	Leviticus 13-15; Luke 15-16

WEEK 8

MONDAY	Leviticus 16-17; Luke 17
TUESDAY	Leviticus 18-19; Luke 18
WEDNESDAY	Leviticus 20-21; Luke 19
THURSDAY	Leviticus 22-23; Luke 20
FRIDAY	Leviticus 24-25; Luke 21
SATURDAY	Leviticus 26-27; Luke 22
SUNDAY	Numbers 1-3; Luke 23-24

WEEK 9

MONDAY	Numbers 4-5; John 1
TUESDAY	Numbers 6-7; John 2
WEDNESDAY	Numbers 8-9; John 3
THURSDAY	Numbers 10-11; John 4
FRIDAY	Numbers 12-13; John 5
SATURDAY	Numbers 14-15; John 6
SUNDAY	Numbers 16-18; John 7-8

WEEK 10

MONDAY	Numbers 19-20; John 9
TUESDAY	Numbers 21-22; John 10
WEDNESDAY	Numbers 23-24; John 11
THURSDAY	Numbers 25-26; John 12
FRIDAY	Numbers 27-28; John 13
SATURDAY	Numbers 29-30; John 14
SUNDAY	Numbers 31-33; John 15-16

WEEK 11

MONDAY	Numbers 34-35; John 17
TUESDAY	Numbers 36-Deuteronomy 1; John 18
WEDNESDAY	Deuteronomy 2-3; John 19
THURSDAY	Deuteronomy 4-5; John 20
FRIDAY	Deuteronomy 6-7; John 21
SATURDAY	Deuteronomy 8-9; Acts 1
SUNDAY	Deuteronomy 10-12; Acts 2-3

WEEK 12

MONDAY	Deuteronomy 13-14; Acts 4
TUESDAY	Deuteronomy 15-16; Acts 5
WEDNESDAY	Deuteronomy 17-18; Acts
THURSDAY	Deuteronomy 19-20; Acts 7
FRIDAY	Deuteronomy 21-22; Acts 8
SATURDAY	Deuteronomy 23-24; Acts 9
SUNDAY	Deuteronomy 25-27; Acts 10-11

WEEK 13

MONDAY	Deuteronomy 28-29; Acts 12
TUESDAY	Deuteronomy 30-31; Acts 13
WEDNESDAY	Deuteronomy 32-33; Acts 14
THURSDAY	Deuteronomy 34-Joshua 1; Acts 15
FRIDAY	Joshua 2-3; Acts 16
SATURDAY	Joshua 4-5; Acts 17
SUNDAY	Joshua 6-8; Acts 18-19

WEEK 14

MONDAY	Joshua 9-10; Acts 20
TUESDAY	Joshua 11-12; Acts 21
WEDNESDAY	Joshua 13-14; Acts 22
THURSDAY	Joshua 15-16; Acts 23
FRIDAY	Joshua 17-18; Acts 24
SATURDAY	Joshua 19-21; Acts 25
SUNDAY	Joshua 22-24; Acts 26-27

WEEK 15

MONDAY	Judges 1-2; Acts 28
TUESDAY	Judges 3-4; Romans 1
WEDNESDAY	Judges 5-6; Romans 2
THURSDAY	Judges 7-8; Romans 3
FRIDAY	Judges 9-10; Romans 4
SATURDAY	Judges 11-12; Romans 5
SUNDAY	Judges 13-15; Romans 6-7

WEEK 16

MONDAY	Judges 16-17; Romans 8
TUESDAY	Judges 18-19; Romans 9
WEDNESDAY	Judges 20-21; Romans 10
THURSDAY	Ruth 1-2; Romans 11
FRIDAY	Ruth 3-4; Romans 12
SATURDAY	1 Samuel 1-2; Romans 13
SUNDAY	1 Samuel 3-5; Romans 14-15

WEEK 17

MONDAY	1 Samuel 6-7; Romans 16
TUESDAY	1 Samuel 8-9; 1 Corinthians 1
WEDNESDAY	1 Samuel 10-11; 1 Corinthians 2
THURSDAY	1 Samuel 12-13; 1 Corinthians 3
FRIDAY	1 Samuel 14-15; 1 Corinthians 4
SATURDAY	1 Samuel 16-17; 1 Corinthians 5
SUNDAY	1 Samuel 18-20; 1 Corinthians 6-7

WEEK 18

MONDAY	1 Samuel 21-22; 1 Corinthians 8
TUESDAY	1 Samuel 23-24; 1 Corinthians 9
WEDNESDAY	1 Samuel 25-26; 1 Corinthians 10
THURSDAY	1 Samuel 27-28; 1 Corinthians 11
FRIDAY	1 Samuel 29-30; 1 Corinthians 12
SATURDAY	1 Samuel 31-2 Samuel 1; 1 Corinthians 13
SUNDAY	2 Samuel 2-4; 1 Corinthians 14-15

WEEK 19

MONDAY	2 Samuel 5-6; 1 Corinthians 16
TUESDAY	2 Samuel 7-8; 2 Corinthians 1
WEDNESDAY	2 Samuel 9-10; 2 Corinthians 2
THURSDAY	2 Samuel 11-12; 2 Corinthians 3
FRIDAY	2 Samuel 13-14; 2 Corinthians 4
SATURDAY	2 Samuel 15-16; 2 Corinthians 5
SUNDAY	2 Samuel 17-19; 2 Corinthians 6-7

WEEK 20

MONDAY	2 Samuel 20-21; 2 Corinthians 8
TUESDAY	2 Samuel 22-23; 2 Corinthians 9
WEDNESDAY	2 Samuel 24-1 Kings 1; 2 Corinthians 10
THURSDAY	1 Kings 2-3; 2 Corinthians 11
FRIDAY	1 Kings 4-5; 2 Corinthians 12
SATURDAY	1 Kings 6-7; 2 Corinthians 13
SUNDAY	1 Kings 8-10; Galatians 1-2

WEEK 21

MONDAY	1 Kings 11-12; Galatians 3
TUESDAY	1 Kings 13-14; Galatians 4
WEDNESDAY	1 Kings 15-16; Galatians 5
THURSDAY	1 Kings 17-18; Galatians 6
FRIDAY	1 Kings 19-20; Ephesians 1
SATURDAY	1 Kings 21-22; Ephesians 2
SUNDAY	2 Kings 1-3; Ephesians 3-4

WEEK 22

MONDAY	2 Kings 4-5; Ephesians 5
TUESDAY	2 Kings 6-7; Ephesians 6
WEDNESDAY	2 Kings 8-9; Philippians 1
THURSDAY	2 Kings 10-11; Philippians 2
FRIDAY	2 Kings 12-13; Philippians 3
SATURDAY	2 Kings 14-15; Philippians 4
SUNDAY	2 Kings 16-18; Colossians 1-2

WEEK 23

MONDAY	2 Kings 19-20; Colossians 3
TUESDAY	2 Kings 21-22; Colossians 4
WEDNESDAY	2 Kings 23-24; 1 Thessalonians 1
THURSDAY	1 Chronicles 1-2; 1 Thessalonians 2
FRIDAY	1 Chronicles 3-4; 1 Thessalonians 3
SATURDAY	1 Chronicles 5-7; 1 Thessalonians 4
SUNDAY	1 Chronicles 8-9; 1 Thessalonians 5

WEEK 24

MONDAY	1 Chronicles 10-11; 2 Thessalonians 1
TUESDAY	1 Chronicles 12-13; 2 Thessalonians 2
WEDNESDAY	1 Chronicles 14-15; 2 Thessalonians 3
THURSDAY	1 Chronicles 16-17; 1 Timothy 1
FRIDAY	1 Chronicles 18-19; 1 Timothy 2
SATURDAY	1 Chronicles 20-22; 1 Timothy 3
SUNDAY	1 Chronicles 23-24; 1 Timothy 4-5

WEEK 25

MONDAY	1 Chronicles 25-26; 1 Timothy 6
TUESDAY	1 Chronicles 27-28; 2 Timothy 1
WEDNESDAY	1 Chronicles 29-2 Chronicles 1; 2 Timothy 2
THURSDAY	2 Chronicles 2-3; 2 Timothy 3
FRIDAY	2 Chronicles 4-5; 2 Timothy 4
SATURDAY	2 Chronicles 6-8; Titus 1
SUNDAY	2 Chronicles 9-10; Titus 2-3

WEEK 26

MONDAY	2 Chronicles 11-12; Philemon
TUESDAY	2 Chronicles 13-14; Hebrews 1
WEDNESDAY	2 Chronicles 15-16; Hebrews 2
THURSDAY	2 Chronicles 17-18; Hebrews 3
FRIDAY	2 Chronicles 19-20; Hebrews 4
SATURDAY	2 Chronicles 21-23; Hebrews 5
SUNDAY	2 Chronicles 24-25; Hebrews 6-7

WEEK 27

MONDAY	2 Chronicles 26-27; Hebrews 8
TUESDAY	2 Chronicles 28-29; Hebrews 9
WEDNESDAY	2 Chronicles 30-31; Hebrews 10
THURSDAY	2 Chronicles 32-33; Hebrews 11
FRIDAY	2 Chronicles 34-35; Hebrews 12
SATURDAY	2 Chronicles 36-Ezra 2; Hebrews 13
SUNDAY	Ezra 3-4; James 1-2

WEEK 28

MONDAY	Ezra 5-6; James 3
TUESDAY	Ezra 7-8; James 4
WEDNESDAY	Ezra 9-10; James 5
THURSDAY	Nehemiah 1-2; 1 Peter 1
FRIDAY	Nehemiah 3-4; 1 Peter 2
SATURDAY	Nehemiah 5-7; 1 Peter 3
SUNDAY	Nehemiah 8-9; 1 Peter 4-5

WEEK 29

MONDAY	Nehemiah 10-11; 2 Peter 1
TUESDAY	Nehemiah 12-13; 2 Peter 2
WEDNESDAY	Esther 1-2; 2 Peter 3
THURSDAY	Esther 3-4; 1 John 1
FRIDAY	Esther 5-6; 1 John 2
SATURDAY	Esther 7-9; 1 John 3
SUNDAY	Esther 10-Job 1; 1 John 4-5

WEEK 30

MONDAY	Job 2-3; 2 John
TUESDAY	Job 4-5; 3 John
WEDNESDAY	Job 6-7; Jude
THURSDAY	Job 8-9; Revelation 1
FRIDAY	Job 10-11; Revelation 2
SATURDAY	Job 12-14; Revelation 3
SUNDAY	Job 15-16; Revelation 4-5

WEEK 31

MONDAY	Job 17-18; Revelation 6
TUESDAY	Job 19-20; Revelation 7
WEDNESDAY	Job 21-22; Revelation 8
THURSDAY	Job 23-24; Revelation 9
FRIDAY	Job 25-26; Revelation 10
SATURDAY	Job 27-29; Revelation 11
SUNDAY	Job 30-31; Revelation 12-13

WEEK 32

MONDAY	Job 32-33; Revelation 14
TUESDAY	Job 34-35; Revelation 15
WEDNESDAY	Job 36-37; Revelation 16
THURSDAY	Job 38-39; Revelation 17
FRIDAY	Job 40-41; Revelation 18
SATURDAY	Job 42-Proverbs 2; Revelation 19
SUNDAY	Proverbs 3-4; Revelation 20-21

WEEK 33

MONDAY	Proverbs 5-6; Revelation 22
TUESDAY	Proverbs 7-8; Revelation 23
WEDNESDAY	Proverbs 9-10; Psalm 1
THURSDAY	Proverbs 11-12; Psalm 2
FRIDAY	Proverbs 13-14; Psalm 3
SATURDAY	Proverbs 15-16; Psalm 4
SUNDAY	Proverbs 17-18; Psalms 5-6

WEEK 34

MONDAY	Proverbs 19-20; Psalm 7
TUESDAY	Proverbs 21-22; Psalm 8
WEDNESDAY	Proverbs 23-24; Psalm 9
THURSDAY	Proverbs 25-26; Psalm 10
FRIDAY	Proverbs 27-28; Psalm 11
SATURDAY	Proverbs 29-31; Psalm 12
SUNDAY	Ecclesiastes 1-2; Psalms 13-14

WEEK 35

MONDAY	Ecclesiastes 3-4; Psalm 15
TUESDAY	Ecclesiastes 5-6; Psalm 16
WEDNESDAY	Ecclesiastes 7-8; Psalm 17
THURSDAY	Ecclesiastes 9-10; Psalm 18
FRIDAY	Ecclesiastes 11-12; Psalm 19
SATURDAY	Song of Solomon 1-2; Psalm 20
SUNDAY	Song of Solomon 3-4; Psalms 21-22

WEEK 36

MONDAY	Song of Solomon 5-6; Psalm 23
TUESDAY	Song of Solomon 7-8; Psalm 24
WEDNESDAY	Isaiah 1-2; Psalm 25
THURSDAY	Isaiah 3-4; Psalm 26
FRIDAY	Isaiah 5-6; Psalm 27
SATURDAY	Isaiah 7-9; Psalm 28
SUNDAY	Isaiah 10-11; Psalms 29-30

WEEK 37

MONDAY	Isaiah 12-13; Psalm 31
TUESDAY	Isaiah 14-15; Psalm 32
WEDNESDAY	Isaiah 16-17; Psalm 33
THURSDAY	Isaiah 18-19; Psalm 34
FRIDAY	Isaiah 20-22; Psalm 35
SATURDAY	Isaiah 23-25; Psalm 36
SUNDAY	Isaiah 26-27; Psalms 37-38

WEEK 38

MONDAY	Isaiah 28-29; Psalm 39
TUESDAY	Isaiah 30-31; Psalm 40
WEDNESDAY	Isaiah 32-33; Psalm 41
THURSDAY	Isaiah 34-35; Psalm 42
FRIDAY	Isaiah 36-37; Psalm 43
SATURDAY	Isaiah 38-40; Psalm 44
SUNDAY	Isaiah 41-42; Psalms 45-46

WEEK 39

MONDAY	Isaiah 43-44; Psalm 47
TUESDAY	Isaiah 45-46; Psalm 48
WEDNESDAY	Isaiah 47-48; Psalm 49
THURSDAY	Isaiah 49-50; Psalm 50
FRIDAY	Isaiah 51-52; Psalm 51
SATURDAY	Isaiah 53-55; Psalm 52
SUNDAY	Isaiah 56-57; Psalms 53-54

WEEK 40

MONDAY	Isaiah 58-59; Psalm 55
TUESDAY	Isaiah 60-61; Psalm 56
WEDNESDAY	Isaiah 62-63; Psalm 57
THURSDAY	Isaiah 64-65; Psalm 58
FRIDAY	Isaiah 66-Jeremiah 1; Psalm 59
SATURDAY	Jeremiah 2-4; Psalm 60
SUNDAY	Jeremiah 5-6; Psalms 61-62

WEEK 41

MONDAY	Jeremiah 7-8; Psalm 63
TUESDAY	Jeremiah 9-10; Psalm 64
WEDNESDAY	Jeremiah 11-12; Psalm 65
THURSDAY	Jeremiah 13-14; Psalm 66
FRIDAY	Jeremiah 15-16; Psalm 67
SATURDAY	Jeremiah 17-19; Psalm 68
SUNDAY	Jeremiah 20-21; Psalms 69-70

WEEK 42

MONDAY	Jeremiah 22-23; Psalm 71
TUESDAY	Jeremiah 24-25; Psalm 72
WEDNESDAY	Jeremiah 26-27; Psalm 73
THURSDAY	Jeremiah 28-29; Psalm 74
FRIDAY	Jeremiah 30-31; Psalm 75
SATURDAY	Jeremiah 32-34; Psalm 76
SUNDAY	Jeremiah 35-36; Psalm 77

WEEK 43

MONDAY	Jeremiah 37-38; Psalm 78
TUESDAY	Jeremiah 39-40; Psalm 79
WEDNESDAY	Jeremiah 41-42; Psalm 80
THURSDAY	Jeremiah 43-44; Psalm 81
FRIDAY	Jeremiah 45-46; Psalm 82
SATURDAY	Jeremiah 47-49; Psalm 83
SUNDAY	Jeremiah 50-51; Psalm 84

WEEK 44

MONDAY	Jeremiah 52-Lamentations 1; Psalm 85
TUESDAY	Lamentations 2-3; Psalm 86
WEDNESDAY	Lamentations 4-5; Psalm 87
THURSDAY	Ezekiel 1-2; Psalm 88
FRIDAY	Ezekiel 3-4; Psalm 89
SATURDAY	Ezekiel 5-7; Psalm 90
SUNDAY	Ezekiel 8-9; Psalm 91

WEEK 45

MONDAY	Ezekiel 10-11; Psalm 92
TUESDAY	Ezekiel 12-13; Psalm 93
WEDNESDAY	Ezekiel 14-15; Psalm 94
THURSDAY	Ezekiel 16-17; Psalm 95
FRIDAY	Ezekiel 18-19; Psalm 96
SATURDAY	Ezekiel 20-22; Psalm 97
SUNDAY	Ezekiel 23-24; Psalm 98

WEEK 46

MONDAY	Ezekiel 25-26; Psalm 99
TUESDAY	Ezekiel 27-28; Psalm 100
WEDNESDAY	Ezekiel 29-30; Psalm 101
THURSDAY	Ezekiel 31-32; Psalm 102
FRIDAY	Ezekiel 33-34; Psalm 103
SATURDAY	Ezekiel 35-37; Psalm 104
SUNDAY	Ezekiel 38-39; Psalm 105

WEEK 47

MONDAY	Ezekiel 40-41; Psalm 106
TUESDAY	Ezekiel 42-43; Psalm 107
WEDNESDAY	Ezekiel 44-45; Psalm 108
THURSDAY	Ezekiel 46-47; Psalm 109
FRIDAY	Ezekiel 48-Daniel 1; Psalm 110
SATURDAY	Daniel 2-4; Psalm 111
SUNDAY	Daniel 5-6; Psalm 112

WEEK 48

MONDAY	Daniel 7-8; Psalm 113
TUESDAY	Daniel 9-10; Psalm 114
WEDNESDAY	Daniel 11-12; Psalm 115
THURSDAY	Hosea 1-2; Psalm 116
FRIDAY	Hosea 3-4; Psalm 117
SATURDAY	Hosea 5-7; Psalm 118
SUNDAY	Hosea 8-9; Psalm 119:1-24

WEEK 49

MONDAY	Hosea 10-11; Psalm 119:25-49
TUESDAY	Hosea 12-13; Psalm 119:50-96
WEDNESDAY	Hosea 14-Joel 1; Psalm 119:97-120
THURSDAY	Joel 2-3; Psalm 119:121-176
FRIDAY	Amos 1-2; Psalm 120
SATURDAY	Amos 3-5; Psalm 121
SUNDAY	Amos 6-7; Psalm 122

WEEK 50

MONDAY	Amos 8-9; Psalm 123
TUESDAY	Obadiah 1-Jonah 1; Psalm 124
WEDNESDAY	Jonah 2-3; Psalm 125
THURSDAY	Jonah 4-Micah 1; Psalm 126
FRIDAY	Micah 2-3; Psalm 127
SATURDAY	Micah 4-6; Psalm 128
SUNDAY	Micah 7-Nahum 1; Psalm 129

WEEK 51

MONDAY	Nahum 1; Psalm 130
TUESDAY	Nahum 2-3; Psalm 131
WEDNESDAY	Habakkuk 1-2; Psalm 132
THURSDAY	Habakkuk 3-Zephaniah 1; Psalm 133
FRIDAY	Zephaniah 2-3; Psalm 134
SATURDAY	Haggai 1-2; Psalm 135
SUNDAY	Zechariah 1-3; Psalm 136

WEEK 52

MONDAY	Zechariah 4-5; Psalms 137-138
TUESDAY	Zechariah 6-7; Psalm 139-140
WEDNESDAY	Zechariah 8-9; Psalm 141-142
THURSDAY	Zechariah 10-12; Psalm 143-144
FRIDAY	Zechariah 13-14; Psalm 145-147
SATURDAY	Malachi 1-2; Psalm 148-149
SUNDAY	Malachi 3-4; Psalm 150

Endnotes

Chapter 1

[1] *Webster's Desk Dictionary of the English Language* (New York: Gramercy Books, 1983), p. 780.

Chapter 3

[1] James E. Strong, "Hebrew and Chaldee Dictionary" in *Strong's Exhaustive Concordance of the Bible* (Nashville: Abingdon Press, 1890) p. 29, entry #1696, s.v. "speaketh," Job 33:14.

[2] Strong, p. 114, entry #7789, s.v. "perceiveth," Job 33:14.

[3] Strong, p. 118, entry #8085, s.v. "hearken," Exodus 15:26.

[4] Strong, p. 10, entry #238, s.v. "ear," Exodus 15:26.

Chapter 8

[1] Strong, p. 99, entry #6754, s.v. "image," Genesis 1:26.

[2] Strong, p. 31, entry #1823, s.v. "likeness," Genesis 1:26.

[3] Strong, p. 12, entry #430, s.v. "God," Genesis 1:26.

[4] Strong, p. 47, entry #3068, s.v. "Lord," Genesis 2:7.

[5] Strong, p. 51, entry #3335, s.v. "formed," Genesis 2:7.

[6] Strong, p. 79, entry #5301, s.v. "breathed," Genesis 2:7.

About the Author

Sarah Bowling is the daughter of Pastor Wallace and Marilyn Hickey. Her God-given gifts for Bible teaching and ministry, sparked by her energy and remarkable level of wisdom, are being enthusiastically received by television audiences and churches throughout the world.

A love for missions was sown at an early age when Sarah traveled extensively with her parents. Since that time, Sarah has made ministry trips to Russia, China, the Philippines, Turkey, Eastern Europe, Sudan, Pakistan, and Great Britain, where she has taught and ministered side-by-side with her mother. Covering the earth with the Word has become a passion in Sarah's life, as she wants to make a real impact on the world for Jesus Christ.

Currently, Sarah Bowling is ministering "Jump-Start Your Heart" clinics to congregations around the country. Designed to breathe new life into the believer's walk with God and to help believers regain their edge spiritually, emotionally, and mentally, the "Jump-Start Your Heart" clinics are a unique opportunity for God to change lives and heal families through the power of the Word and confirming miracles.

Sarah and her husband, Reece, live in Denver, Colorado, where they are on staff at Marilyn Hickey Ministries/Orchard Road Christian Center.

To contact Sarah Bowling
write:

Marilyn Hickey Ministries
P.O. Box 17340
Denver, Colorado 80217

*Please include your prayer requests
and comments when you write.*

Additional copies of this book
are available from your local bookstore.

HARRISON HOUSE
Tulsa, Oklahoma 74153

Prayer of Salvation

A born-again, committed relationship with God is the key to a victorious life. Jesus, the Son of God, laid down His life and rose again so that we could spend eternity with Him in heaven and experience His absolute best on earth. The Bible says, **"For God so loved the world, that he gave his only begotten Son, that whosoever believeth in him should not perish, but have everlasting life"** (John 3:16).

It is the will of God that everyone receive eternal salvation. The way to receive this salvation is to call upon the name of Jesus and confess Him as your Lord. The Bible says, **"That if thou shalt confess with thy mouth the Lord Jesus, and shalt believe in thine heart that God hath raised him from the dead, thou shalt be saved. For whosoever shall call upon the name of the Lord shall be saved"** (Romans 10:9,13).

Jesus has given salvation, healing, and countless benefits to all who call upon His name. These benefits can be yours if you receive Him into your heart by praying this prayer:

Heavenly Father, I come to You admitting that I am a sinner.
Right now, I choose to turn away from sin, and I ask You to
cleanse me of all unrighteousness. I believe that Your Son,
Jesus, died on the cross to take away my sins. I also believe
that He rose again from the dead so that I may be justified and
made righteous through faith in Him. I call upon the name of
Jesus Christ to be the Savior and Lord of my life. Jesus, I
choose to follow You, and I ask that You fill me with the power
of the Holy Spirit. I declare right now that I am a born-again
child of God. I am free from sin, and full of the righteousness
of God. I am saved in Jesus' name, Amen.

If you have prayed this prayer to receive Jesus Christ as your
Savior, or if this book has changed your life, we would like to
hear from you. Please write us at:

Harrison House Publishers
P.O. Box 35035
Tulsa, Oklahoma 74153

You can also visit us on the web at
www.harrisonhouse.com

The Harrison House Vision

Proclaiming the truth and the power
Of the Gospel of Jesus Christ
With excellence;

Challenging Christians to
Live victoriously,
Grow spiritually,
Know God intimately.